Vilnius
with Kaunas

THE BRADT CITY GUIDE

Howard Jarvis
Neil Taylor

Bradt Travel Guides Ltd, UK
The Globe Pequot Press Inc, USA

First published April 2006

Bradt Travel Guides Ltd
23 High Street, Chalfont St Peter, Bucks SL9 9QE, England; www.bradtguides.com
Published in the USA by The Globe Pequot Press Inc, 246 Goose Lane, PO Box 480,
Guilford, Connecticut 06437-0480

Text copyright © 2006 Howard Jarvis & Neil Taylor
Maps copyright © 2006 Bradt Travel Guides Ltd
Illustrations © 2006 Individual photographers and artists

A catalogue record for this book is available from the British Library

ISBN-10: 1 84162 112 9
ISBN-13: 978 1 84162 112 8

Front cover Gedimino Prospektas Street and Vilnius Cathedral (Reinhard Schmidt/Fototeca 9x12)
Text photographs Gediminas Treciokas, Baltic Images (GT), Dr Christian Nowak (CN)
Maps Steve Munns *Illustrations* Carole Vincer, Dave Colton

Typeset from the authors' disc by Wakewing
Printed and bound in Spain by Grafo SA, Bilbao

Authors

Neil Taylor was a director from 1975 to 2005 of Regent Holidays, a British tour company that has specialised in travel to the Baltic states since they regained their independence in 1991. He visits the region about six times a year, catching up with the constant changes and raiding all the bookshops to add to his already enormous collection on the Baltics. He also writes and broadcasts on travel-trade topics and teaches on tourism courses at a number of universities. In 2000, he won the Lifetime Achievement Award from the British Guild of Travel Writers for his work in opening up the former communist world to tourism.

Howard Jarvis has been the chief editor of a number of publications in the Baltic countries, including the region's only weekly English-language newspaper, the *Baltic Times*, and the travel-trade magazine, *Baltic Stand By*. He has been a contributor at Jane's Information Group since 2000 and has written numerous articles on developments in the Baltic region and Belarus. Now based in Vilnius he is the editor of a monthly magazine for business travellers called *VilniusNOW!* while still finding a little time for freelance work.

Contents

Contents

Acknowledgements

Howard Jarvis would like to thank Lina Stašinskaitė for her invaluable comments on some of the city's churches and museums, and also for allowing him to exploit her encyclopaedic knowledge of Vilnius and Trakai. Similarly, Albina Trečiokaitė deserves our gratitude for her constant support in this project and the enthusiasm and commitment she shows to her English-speaking group who have the good fortune to experience Lithuania in her company.

FEEDBACK REQUEST

It doesn't matter how well we know Vilnius, every time we look there is always something new to entice the visitor. If you would like to share your comments about places we have mentioned in the guide, or tell us about something new that you have discovered, please do drop us a line at Bradt Travel Guides, 23 High Street, Chalfont St Peter, Bucks SL9 9QE.

Introduction

Lithuania is a Baltic state and Vilnius is its capital. Yet Vilnius is unlike the other 'Baltic capitals' in a number of ways. It is 200 miles from the Baltic Sea and its true links have always been south and west. Links to the north and east have always been imposed, and never voluntarily undertaken. It has in its past been the capital of much more than what is now Lithuania; in the 15th century its boundaries stretched to the Black Sea and the country was 18 times as large as that within its current borders. In later centuries it has suffered as much as Riga and Tallinn, but usually under different occupiers and at different times. Only World War II and the subsequent occupation forced an artificial bond over the three capitals.

If you catch Vilnius on a hot summer's day, you may feel as though you are in southern Europe rather than in the north, with light pastel colours on most façades in the Old Town and an exuberant Baroque church staring out from every corner. Shade can be as important as sunshine. Wine is as perfectly natural to drink here as beer, and it is not essential to race back to work after lunch.

The Tsarist and then Soviet rulers from Russia have left an architectural legacy, but it is fortunately far less obvious in the town centre than in Warsaw, Riga, Tallinn or in the other major Lithuanian cities. Like the people, the architecture is sedate.

The 19th- and 20th-century political, religious and military history of Vilnius has been well concealed and perhaps this is just as well; only since 1990 have the population been aware of it. In 1985 three researchers rediscovered the Vilnius

Cathedral Treasury that had been hidden since 1939. So frightened were they that the treasures would be taken to Moscow, that only in 1998, when they felt absolutely certain of Lithuanian independence, did they reveal their discovery.

Preliminary work for a new bridge across the Neris which was started in 2000 revealed a hoard of coins that had been hidden from the Swedes before their occupation of Vilnius in 1702. In 2001 two different mounds of bones were discovered; one was from the French soldiers who died in Vilnius during the retreat from Moscow in 1812 and the other from Russian soldiers killed in the recapture of the city from the Germans in 1944. By 2003, excavations revealed the execution chambers at the KGB headquarters where hundreds of Lithuanian patriots were secretly killed in the late 1940s. A few years earlier the Nazis had carried out their executions in the forest at Paneriai, sufficiently far from the town not to be seen and where the evidence could be more easily concealed.

The most recent tragedy to take place in Vilnius was on 13 January 1991 when the Soviet army killed unarmed civilians guarding the Television Tower. This was in front of the world's media and the exposure has probably ensured that Lithuanian independence will never be threatened again. Contemporary Vilnius fights its internal political battles through the media and no longer on the streets. A whole generation has now grown up with no recollection of this past, or of queues, censorship or military service in distant parts of the USSR. Tourists can ignore this past if they wish, but will probably be able to appreciate the present more if they realise the background against which it has arisen.

Fortunately contemporary Vilnius now shows off rather than hides. Tourists may wear torn jeans at an opera or be happy to drive a car 20 years old. Do not expect such behaviour from local people. At 15.00 in an office or at 03.00 in a nightclub, expect them to take care about their appearance and similar care about their surroundings. If you witness raucous behaviour late at night, it will be from tourists taking advantage of the cheap beer, not locals on a regular weekend binge.

In early 2005, Vilnius was awarded the accolade of European Capital of Culture for 2009, which it will share with Linz as the award will by then be shared between a city in 'old' Europe and one in the 'accession' states. Yet Vilnius is as 'old' and as 'European' as any other contenders for this award, in fact in many respects more so. Younger visitors will find it hard to believe that from 1945 until 1990, the only way to travel abroad from Vilnius was by plane via Moscow and that this was a privilege granted to very few local people indeed. The few foreigners who came in the other direction were allowed only three nights there, in case they stayed long enough to 'contaminate' the local population with counter-revolutionary thoughts. Travel outside the city was forbidden.

Now Vilnius is firmly back where it belongs. There are four flights a day to London, but only one a day to Moscow. Dozens of coaches a day drive tourists, students and labourers to Poland and Germany. Very few bother to drive the 100 miles east to Minsk, or the rather longer distances to Kaliningrad or St Petersburg. It is almost impossible to find goods produced in Russia in the shops.

Visitors who delay their visit to Vilnius until the end of the decade will see some

Introduction

of the few aspects of Western life which were still missing in 2005. In the outskirts, garden cities will slowly replace blocks of flats. Skyscrapers there will certainly be, and some were completed as early as 2004, including the shiny new town hall over the river from the Old Town. It will soon just be one of many, as a former sleazy area of town becomes the business centre of the whole country. Stricter parking regulations in the Old Town will give more space to pedestrians. Commuters will come in on smooth-running trams rather than on bumpy trolleybuses. A town bypass will have removed unnecessary lorries from the suburbs and some of the smart Old Town restaurants will have moved to the shopping malls which cater to the burgeoning middle classes. What visitors really want, however, is going to remain – a different walk on their doorstep whenever they leave a hotel, cuisine from any country in Europe that can claim to have one, a choice of music every night from the most reverential to the most outrageous and an artistic legacy as strong in the façades of its buildings as what they display inside.

Visitors are unlikely to see any signs in Polish or Russian. Lithuanian has finally become the dominant language, which shows how far in the past the role of these former masters is. When the local shops start to take the euro, likely to be in 2008, the country's policy of closer integration with its Western neighbours will, for the first time in centuries, have been decided in Vilnius, and not in Moscow, Warsaw, Paris or Berlin.

How to use this book

Email addresses Where an email address is given, assume that correspondence in English is fine.

Websites In this book it can be assumed that if a website address is given, it has an English text. This certainly applies to hotels and restaurants. Many restaurants give their menus on a website.

Map references These relate to the colour map section at the end of the guide.

Hotel prices These fluctuate wildly according to which agency is used for the booking, the time of year and the day of the week. Luxury hotels tend to charge more in the winter and mid-week, as they cater then for business visitors. Cheaper hotels operate on the reverse principle as most of their clients come at weekends and during the summer. Prices given should be taken only as a rough guide. No large new hotels are expected in 2006, but in 2007 there will probably be another thousand rooms in Vilnius, which should lead to lower prices. Unless otherwise stated, room prices include a buffet breakfast and all taxes.

Restaurant prices These always include VAT but rarely service. Adding 10% for good service is to be recommended but do not do this if the service is surly.

Kompleksiniai pietūs (fixed price menus) are now quite common at lunchtime, usually consisting of soup and a main dish. For their à la carte menus, most restaurants charge the same for lunch and dinner. Whilst prices for food and beer are usually reasonable, those for wine vary a lot so do check them before ordering a bottle.

Restaurant opening hours Restaurants tend to open at 11.00 and not to close during the afternoon. People in Lithuania eat when they are hungry rather than when they feel it is an appropriate time. Booking in advance is rare, much as restaurants would like to claim otherwise. There is an enormous choice of good restaurants in and near the Old Town. The suburbs remain gastronomically bleak, so there is no point in searching there! All restaurants now have menus in English.

Café opening hours Not many cafés open for breakfast as this meal is included in hotel prices and the American idea of a business breakfast has not yet caught on in Vilnius. Once they open at 10.00 or so, they divide into those that close around 18.00 and those likely to stay open throughout the evening. The latter are usually bigger and have a wider choice of food. Whilst a few pubs on the English and Irish model have opened in Vilnius, cafés and bars tend to be combined, being just as happy to serve beer and vodka as tea or coffee.

Museum opening hours Museums still open to suit the staff rather than the needs of visitors. Even in the peak summer season, most close one day a week and some close on two. These days tend to be Mondays and Tuesdays. They do not usually bother to open until 11.00 and close on the dot of 17.00. On public holidays, it is important to check what their opening hours are as this can vary from year to year and museum to museum. Expect to pay an admission charge of between 2Lt and 5Lt. Tour operators can usually arrange with the smaller museums to open at other times for groups but the admission charge may then well be higher.

How to use this book

VILNIUS AT A GLANCE

Location Vilnius is the capital of Lithuania, the southernmost of the three Baltic states, located in the southwest of the country about 200 miles from the Baltic coast and less than 20 miles from the border with Belarus. Flights from London take just under three hours. Nearby cities such as Warsaw, Riga, Tallinn and Helsinki can easily be reached by plane or bus.

Population 553,000

Language Lithuanian (you'll also hear Russian and Polish)

Religion Catholic

Time GMT +2 hours, as in the other Baltic countries

International telephone code +370

Currency Litas (Lt)

Exchange rate $1 = 2.9Lt, £1= 5Lt, €1 = 3.45Lt

Electricity 220v; two-pin plugs

Public holidays 1 January, 16 February, 11 March, 1 May, 24 June, 6 July, 25/6 December

School holidays Mid-July to late August; short breaks at Christmas and Easter

Climate Daytime temperatures Nov–Feb minus 10–0°C; Mar–May, Sep–Oct 5–15°C; Jun–Aug 20–30°C.

Contents

HISTORY

The main avenue in Vilnius has had several names over the past 100 years – Stalin Avenue, Lenin Avenue and, under the tsars, St George's Avenue, to name but three. The current name, Gedimino Avenue, is, of course, the only appropriate one, being in honour of the man considered to be the founder of the city, Grand Duke Gediminas. The place where the bubbling little River Vilnia meets the broad River Neris is known to have been inhabited since at least the Bronze Age. We know that in the 11th century a castle made of wood stood where the Higher Castle now stands. But it was Gediminas who provided the first known written record of the city, in a letter dated 1323 inviting German merchants, craftsmen and farmers to settle in and around his city, which he had raised to the status of capital, offering them exemption from taxes and freedom of worship.

A popular local legend about the birth of Vilnius tells how Gediminas was on a hunting trip with his entourage around these heavily wooded hills when he decided to set up camp rather than return to his castle at Trakai. During the night he dreamed of a huge iron wolf standing on the hill, howling the howl of a hundred wolves. He consulted a pagan priest about the dream, who told him that it was a sign to build a great fortress and city there. The howling meant that the future city's fame would spread far and wide.

In truth, it was certainly Gediminas who transferred the court from Trakai to

Vilnius around the year 1320. At the time Vilnius was already a bustling trading centre with German and Russian communities who had their own churches, even though the country itself remained pagan. The Teutonic Order made frequent and bloody raids on the country, but Gediminas managed to put off any major incursions by promising repeatedly to convert to Christianity – which he never did. While he procrastinated with the West, he expanded the emerging Lithuanian empire to the south and east as far as Ukraine.

In time the threat from the Crusaders became more acute; Vilnius was attacked seven times between 1365 and 1402. More protective fortifications and two more castles were built. The pagan state finally succumbed to Christian conversion when Grand Duke Jogaila initiated a 400-year common history between Lithuania and Poland through marriage. This failed to stop the relentless assaults of Teutonic Knights, however, and it was not until the Battle of Žalgiris in 1410 that Grand Duke Vytautas dealt them a blow from which they never recovered. Vytautas also annexed many Ukrainian and Russian lands, pushing the Lithuanian empire all the way to shores of the Black Sea.

Vilnius flourished for the next 200 years, in a period of growth and prosperity it has never seen since. New roads extended the city in all directions, while Slavs, Jews and Tatars settled in large numbers. The city's first synagogue was built in the 16th century. The Union of Lublin in 1569 further strengthened the bond with Poland, creating a huge unified state, or commonwealth. Vilnius lost its administrative role and Polish dominated as the official language, but the arrival of the Jesuits that same year resulted in a construction boom in the new Baroque style of architecture, much of it sponsored by a small number of powerful noble families. A college that the Jesuits founded became a university in 1579, which soon earned itself a reputation as one of Europe's great academic institutions. Meanwhile, the role played by the Roman Catholic Church in the life of the city strengthened.

War and plague followed, however, bringing destruction and decline to this city of 30,000. As the might of Muscovy grew, the commonwealth failed to hold off a powerful invasion in 1655. Cossacks plundered Vilnius for weeks, destroying Catholic and Jewish buildings, wreaking anarchy and terrorising inhabitants. Almost half of the city's population was lost to plague which hit the city in 1657–58, while the rampaging Russians were not driven out until 1660. But, surprisingly, Vilnius recovered quickly. Magnificent Baroque churches, chapels, mansions and palaces were built over the coming decades and, despite the city being attacked and occupied by both Russian and Swedish armies in the early 18th century, as well as being devastated by more fires and plague, many have survived to this day.

The long, steady decline of the Polish–Lithuanian Commonwealth resulted in a third and final partition in 1795, in which Vilnius, now a city of 20,000, and most of Lithuania became part of Tsarist Russia. Hopes for independence were briefly revived when Napoleon stormed through Europe and captured Vilnius in 1812 and in the 19 days he spent in the city he set up a provisional national government. But, six months later, a decrepit Grand Armée, beaten at Berezina and frozen by the Russian winter, staggered back to Vilnius with mounted Cossacks hot on their heels.

Some 40,000 of Napoleon's soldiers died in Vilnius from starvation, cold or under the Cossacks' swords, most of them bundled into mass graves and church crypts.

The people of Vilnius continued to struggle for independence. Resistance was especially rife at Vilnius University, which paid a harsh penalty for its participation in a rebellion in 1831. It was closed the following year, a measure that would stay in effect right up until Lithuania finally won back its freedom 90 years later. Catholic churches were closed or converted to the Russian Orthodox faith. The Russian authorities even considered changing the name of the city to Chortovgorod ('city of devils'). After hanging the rebels of a second rebellion in 1864 on Lukiškių Square, a ban was imposed on written Lithuanian and street names were changed to Russian ones.

Like other European cities, Vilnius now thrived as a zone of industry. Its population swelled to more than 150,000 by the end of the 19th century, with Russians arriving in large numbers. The city also thrived as a centre of Jewish culture and learning in Yiddish, becoming known as the 'Jerusalem of the North', though the community remained very much cut off from the rest of society. The proportion of Lithuanians shrank, so that by 1904 the authorities could see no danger in lifting the ban on their language. Books, newspapers and cultural organisations quickly encouraged national awareness at a time when feelings of national identity were on the rise throughout Europe. In December 1905, a 'Great Seimas' of 2,000 Lithuanians demanded greater autonomy and the use of Lithuanian in schools. The latter demand was granted.

Nine years later war was once again unleashed on Europe. The mighty German army stormed eastwards and in late 1915 the Russians abandoned Vilnius, which now had a population of 235,000. A new Lithuanian Council was formed, which began negotiations with the Germans for full independence, a goal that was reached in a declaration on 16 February 1918. Chaos reigned, however, and in the scuffles at the end of the war the Bolshevik army and the Polish army each held the city twice and Lithuania once. Lithuania's possession of the city was agreed to on all sides on 7 October 1920, but two days later the Polish army marched north and retook it, an action secretly backed by the Polish leader Jozef Pilsudski, who had been born near Vilnius. When Pilsudski died 15 years later, his wishes were that his body should be buried in Warsaw, but that his heart should be cut out and buried in Vilnius. His heart lies today encased in his mother's tomb in Rasų Cemetery.

After a period of lacklustre international mediation, the League of Nations put Vilnius on the Polish side of a demarcation line in 1922. Lithuania protested by stressing the city's historic role as its former capital, but its appeals fell on deaf ears. In a characteristic display of persistence, the newly independent nation retaliated early in 1923 by seizing Memel (Klaipėda), then under League of Nations supervision, giving it a vitally needed port on the Baltic Sea. Under Polish control, Vilnius's economy and importance declined while Kanuas developed quickly as the new Lithuanian capital. Lithuanian cultural activities in Vilnius were curbed, mass was allowed only in Polish and many ethnic Lithuanians moved to Kaunas.

History

In March 1939, Hitler was given his last bloodless conquest when Nazi Germany took Klaipėda. The carve-up of eastern Europe that resulted from the Molotov–Ribbentrop Pact of 23 August 1939 initially consigned a helpless Lithuania to the German sphere of influence. But when Lithuania refused to attack Poland as a German ally, a second secret pact signed in Moscow on 27 September transferred it to the Soviet sphere. On 10 October, while Soviet military bases were being established within the country, Vilnius was returned to Lithuania. Occupation, then annexation, followed in June 1940. On 14 June 1941 the first Soviet deportations were carried out and 35,000 people were sent to the frozen wastes of Siberia. Most did not survive the first winter.

On 22 June the Nazis surprised Stalin by launching Operation Barbarossa. Within two days they were in Vilnius. With the Nazi occupation of 1941–44 came the murder of 95% of the country's pre-war Jewish population of 300,000 people. Since Jews made up 40% of the population of Vilnius, this meant that virtually half the city was systematically eliminated, mostly in the Paneriai Forest close to the city. Only one German officer rebelled against this policy, Major Karl Plagge, who probably saved about 1,000 Jews during this time. In April 2005 he was posthumously awarded Israel's 'Righteous Amongst the Nations' honour for his courage.

The war ended with a second Soviet occupation of Vilnius, one that was to last almost 50 years. Demographic changes continued. Tens of thousands of Lithuanians had fled westwards to escape the clutches of the Soviets. With Vilnius now in the

Soviet Union, many Poles moved west and there were further deportations to Siberia – about 130,000 between 1944 and 1953, including a third of the clergy. Armed resistance and guerilla warfare took place against Soviet rule throughout the Baltic countries, but by Stalin's death in 1953 this had been brutally crushed. However, as more Russians and migrant Lithuanians arrived in Vilnius, the city's population started to grow again.

Vilnius remained the capital of occupied Lithuania. Churches were closed to become warehouses and car repair garages, then later, during the Krushchev era, some became art galleries and museums. Grey suburbs of factory-made housing blocks were constructed for the growing numbers of workers. Most Lithuanians managed to find work within the system, whether in collective farming on nationalised land or in the industrialised city. Initially, the institutions of power such as the Communist Party, the government and the KGB, were in Russian hands, but gradually, as the years passed, more and more college graduates joined the Party knowing that this would further their careers. However, underground publications also began to appear, particularly in the 1970s, the most significant being the *Chronicle of the Catholic Church in Lithuania*. It was smuggled abroad under the noses of the KGB for 20 years and was never discovered.

When Mikhail Gorbachev tried to stop the stagnation of the Brezhnev years by introducing greater openness, a group of Lithuanian cultural figures and academics set up the Sąjūdis national movement in 1988 to push for further discussion about the past. As popular support quickly grew, its leaders began to speak of

THE TRAGIC RETREAT OF NAPOLEON'S GREAT ARMY
Napoleon's orders before setting off for France were that Vilnius should be held against the advancing Russians. But the demoralised remnants of the once-mighty Grand Armée were in no fit state to defend anything. Already shattered by defeat at Berezina, the retreat towards Vilnius through temperatures reaching −37°C was a tragedy.

Thousands of soldiers suffered from frostbite and snowblindness. Contorted frozen corpses lined the way. Many succumbed to the cold as they walked, staggering for a few metres before falling dead. Only the promise of shelter at Vilnius kept the surviving soldiers going. But when they finally reached the Gates of Dawn, the narrow southern entrance to the city, on 9 December, a bottleneck of men, horses, wagons, carts and improvised sledges built up; many were crushed to death as the desperate rabble pushed from behind. Those who escaped staggered to cafés and private houses to beg for shelter and something to eat.

Locals did what they could to help. Monasteries and churches were used as barracks and makeshift hospitals. Many soldiers were so relieved at being able to rest that they barely felt their toenails come away as they took off their boots. However, panic swept through Vilnius the following morning when word spread that the Cossacks were approaching. Ignoring Napoleon's order to defend the city, the fragmented army struggled to organise an orderly departure. But men and horses slipped on the icy sloping streets of the old city, and wagons and carts crashed into each other.

Most of the locals refused to help, now fearing reprisals from the avenging Russians. In an episode from Adam Zamoyski's graphic retelling of Napoleon's Russian campaign, *1812: Napoleon's Fatal March on Moscow*, Major Jean Noel, who had come from the opposite direction bringing batteries of guns from Germany, was amazed to meet waves of fugitives, together with the carriage of Joachim Murat, King of Naples, whom Napoleon had put in charge in his place.

After introducing himself, Noel asked what his orders were. 'Major, we are f****d,' came the reply. 'Get on your horse and run.' The final act in the tragedy of the retreat through Vilnius was about to unfold. At Paneriai, the road west towards Kaunas rises amid thick forest up a steep hill. But there was no sand laid to prevent slippage on the ice and chaos ensued as the soldiers attempted the ascent. Carriages and carts slid backwards, often picking up speed and pulverising anything in their way. Horses fell, and the artillery had to be abandoned. Looting soldiers ransacked the army treasury when it too was left behind. But this was to be their last action. Mounted Cossacks appeared and hacked the looters down, before they too helped themselves.

A DESCRIPTION OF VILNIUS IN 1924

Late in the evening of 21 June 1924, I arrived in Vilna. It was the eve of St John's Day, the great pagan midsummer festival throughout the Baltics.

Fires were lit beside the river, small boats decorated with lanterns and bearing festive parties were rowed up and down stream. The sound of music and singing floated over the water. From the midst of the city, outlined against the pale northern sky, rose abruptly the Hill of Gedimin like an altar to the ancient gods of the Lithuanian race.

Vilna is now, by the turn of the international kaleidoscope, part of the Republic of Poland, but there has been no revolutionary change in social manners. The old formalities of address still continue. The hotel porter and the barefooted chambermaid both addressed me as 'Barin' or lord. 'Would the Barin like some hot water? Will the Barin be wearing his coat?' It is an old, old word in Vilna.

My hotel was in Adam Mickiewicz Street, named after the national poet of

independence, a full declaration of which came on 11 March 1990. Lithuania was the first Soviet republic to do so.

The move was met by Moscow imposing a tense economic blockade. Then, while the attention of the world was focused on the Gulf, came a night of

Poland who was a native of Lithuania and a student at the University of Vilna. The next street on the right was Jagellon Street, named after the Grand Duke who united the thrones of Lithuania and Poland.

I passed a 'Kultur' shop, in the window of which was displayed a large map showing the extent of the former territories of Poland and Lithuania, stretching from the Baltic to the Black Sea. The new generation in Vilna feeds its soul upon dreams of the past.

Some day Europe will rediscover Vilna. At present, few people in Western Europe know that this is a bone of contention between Poland and Lithuania and that it is impossible to make out whether it is inhabited by Poles, Lithuanians, Russians or Jews. To discover Vilna is to revisit an ancient civilisation which has for centuries been buried under the debris of later and barbarous regimes. However the Vilna that now emerges is no city of the dead. Europe must learn that Vilna has a personality and that it is a very vivid one.

From Beyond The Baltic *by A MacCullum Scott, published in 1925.*

orchestrated violence as Soviet tanks ran through a crowd of unarmed Lithuanian civilians protecting the Vilnius Television Tower on 13 January 1991, resulting in 14 deaths.

Three weeks later, Iceland became the first country of many to recognise

History

Lithuanian independence. The crumbling Soviet empire fell that August.

Once again Vilnius is the proud capital of an independent country that is today part of the European Union and NATO. Since independence, a succession of dynamic, at times controversial mayors has generated local, national and international funds to restore the Old Town, which was declared a UNESCO World Heritage Site in 1994. Since 2003 a new city of glass-fronted skyscrapers has risen over the river. Whilst friends of Vilnius would argue that the city's selection for the coveted European Capital of Culture award for 2009 was an obvious choice, this did not come about without the serious and long-term planning put into the town's submission by the municipal authorities. The private sector too has shown its confidence in Vilnius. Hardly any major Western company does not have representation there and the number of outside investors in the hotel and construction businesses shows a long-term worldwide commitment to its continuing success.

Dates in the history of Vilnius

1323   First documentary mention of Vilnius
1572   Opening of first synagogue in Vilnius
1579   Founding of Vilnius University
1610   Fire destroys most of the city
1795   Vilnius absorbed into Tsarist Russian Empire; population 20,000
1812   City briefly occupied by French troops as they advanced to and then retreated from Moscow

1832	Closure of the university by Tsar Nicholas I; it would not open again until 1919
1864	Obligatory use of the Cyrillic alphabet for writing Lithuanian
1895	Population reaches 150,000
1904	Use of Roman alphabet for writing Lithuanian again permitted
1915	German army occupies Vilnius
1918–20	Vilnius is a battleground between the Germans, Lithuanians, Poles and Soviet Russians.
1918	(16 Feb) Signing in Vilnius of declaration of independence of Lithuania
1919	(11 Oct) University reopens
1920	(9 Oct) Polish army seizes Vilnius and holds it for 19 years
1939	(29 Oct) Vilnius briefly returned to Lithuania by Soviet government
1940	(15 Jun) Vilnius occupied by Soviet troops as Lithuania is incorporated into the USSR
1941	(25 Jun) Vilnius occupied by Nazi forces
1944	(7 Jul) Vilnius reoccupied by Soviet troops
1956	Statues of Stalin removed throughout Lithuania
1987	(23 Aug) First major public demonstration in Vilnius held by Lithuanian Freedom League
1989	(23 Aug) Start of 'Baltic Chain' at Vilnius Cathedral with two million people holding hands from there to Tallinn
1990	(11 Mar) Restoration of Lithuanian independence proclaimed

History

1991	(13 Jan) Soviet troops kill 14 people while storming the Television Tower
1991	(21 Aug) Collapse of Moscow putsch ensures worldwide recognition of Lithuanian independence.
1993	(31 Aug) Last Soviet troops leave Vilnius (4 Sep) Visit of Pope John Paul II
2004	(2 Apr) Lithuania joins NATO (1 May) Lithuania joins the EU
2005	Vilnius is designated (joint) European Capital of Culture for 2009

POLITICS

Vilnius has been fortunate that for much of the time since independence was re-established in 1991, it has had a strong mayor able to formulate policies and get them implemented. Whilst the councils in Tallinn and Riga remain faction-ridden and therefore prone to indecision, Vilnius gives the impression of knowing where it will be next week, next year and in the next decade. Business is being encouraged out of the Old Town over the river into the new business centre being created from the former urban wilderness of Šnipškės. Visitors who came in summer 2004 were surprised to see the sudden arrival of a beach along the river, with sand from Lithuania's coastal dunes brought in on trucks. The main avenue, Gedimino, is now a pedestrian precinct in the evening hours, and great resources are being found for restoration of old buildings. Traffic in the Old Town remains a problem while too many important (or self-important) people who want to park there prevent restrictions from being implemented. The need to be ready for 2009, when Vilnius is joint European Capital of Culture, is bound to keep the current pace going.

Contexts

ECONOMY AND BUSINESS

After the collapse of the USSR in the early 1990s, the transfer from the command economy to a capitalist one was carried out in Lithuania more slowly than in some of the other eastern European countries, and probably less painfully as a result. Unlike in Estonia, Hungary or Slovenia, there had never been an affluent neighbour offering an economic model which seemed instantly tempting. Equally attempts by Moscow to inflict on Lithuania the polluting factories that blighted most other countries in eastern Europe were successfully resisted by the local communist leadership. The economy has therefore been largely based on agriculture, but the emphasis on light industry such as textiles and furniture is leading to diversification.

Privatisation has been undertaken with less urgency than in some neighbouring countries, but most large companies are now in private hands. EU membership and commitment to the euro has taken much of the economic decision-making away from Vilnius, a policy position that was endorsed by 91% of those who voted in the 2003 referendum. Incomes and therefore most prices remain low in comparison with western Europe, an average salary in 2006 being around £300/US$550 a month, but they are increasing.

Lithuania will continue to suffer in the foreseeable future from its two erratic neighbours, the Kaliningrad oblast and Belarus, both sources of cheap uncontrolled labour and of serious smuggling. After EU accession, some brave Lithuanian companies tried to take advantage of these lower labour costs in Kaliningrad by transferring production there. It has to be said that Lithuania certainly benefits from its massive

ARTŪRAS ZUOKAS, THE SKYSCRAPER MAYOR

What an overwhelming feeling of change there is in the Lithuanian capital these days. The Old Town, once notable for its elegant ruins, left to gently crumble during decades of neglect in the Soviet era, is now the centre of a storm of activity. On the other side of the river, a series of brand new, shiny skyscrapers stand above a broad boulevard known as the local Champs-Elysées. Vilnius is suddenly looking like a modern European capital you can do business in.

It would be a mistake to suggest that all these developments are down to one man's will. But the youthful, energetic mayor of Vilnius, Artūras Zuokas, elected in April 2000, is especially keen on raising the city's profile. He is determined to transform the sleepy Lithuanian capital into the Baltic region's most technologically advanced financial, business and cultural centre.

That dream will take some persistence before it can be realised. Like many of Lithuania's leading politicians, Mr Zuokas has been accused of corruption and is faced with ongoing court cases. But he is showing no signs of giving up. He brushes off accusations of both bribery and alleged attempts to influence the outcome of his re-election in 2003 as being politically motivated. It has always been easy to make enemies in Lithuania's shady world of politics and business.

With a background in television journalism – he was a war correspondent in the 1990s in Iraq, Iran and Chechnya – Artūras Zuokas could see how easy it was to lobby the world's big television networks to get his city on the weather maps. It was, for a while, until the mayors and authorities of other neighbouring capitals got the same idea. Head of the Liberal-Centrist Union, one of the country's biggest political parties, his business breakfasts became forums for discussing problems facing businesspeople from all walks of life.

Away from the new skyscrapers, the Old Town has been quietly and elegantly patched up. The splashes of pastel colours began before Mr Zuokas's tenure, but are now adorning the once rundown buildings of Užupis, the atmospheric district that the mayor has made his home.

But taking into account the various patches of wasteland in the Old Town that could be regenerated into prime real estate, Mr Zuokas thinks that even this peaceful haven of the city needs a more dynamic edge. Controversially, he gave the go-ahead to plans to build a business centre on top of the cellars of what used to be a bustling row of houses in the old Jewish quarter. UNESCO, which eagerly awarded the Old Town World Heritage Site status ten years ago, has threatened to withdraw that decision.

Any attempts to balance the quaintly old-fashioned with glass-fronted modernity are bound to lead to arguments. Sympathisers with the mayor claim that at least he comes up with original ideas and tries them out rather than resorting to endless debates.

Economy and business

imports of amber from Kaliningrad, used not only to tempt tourists in Vilnius Old Town, but also as a medicine and in some small-scale industrial production.

It has not been difficult to promote Vilnius as a tourism destination, since its appeal is so varied. The diaspora from several generations is eager to come home, having been so cut off for 50 years. Many returners are involved in charitable work and in setting up small businesses. The size of Vilnius makes it very convenient for a city break as most attractions are within walking distance of the major hotels. Visas were quickly abolished or procedures greatly simplified for most Europeans very soon after independence and investment in hotels has clearly paid off for those who started early.

Geographers in the early '90s conveniently (for Lithuania) discovered that the centre of Europe in fact lay very close to Vilnius, being halfway between the west coast of Ireland and the Urals. For a time, this was merely viewed as a curiosity to promote to tourists, but as Vilnius now looks beyond tourism to a role as a conference and business centre, this location will be a major element in its advertising. The city council is happy to point out that within a catchment area of 300km around Vilnius, there is a population of 15.5 million whereas the comparable figure for St Petersburg is 4 million and for Riga 8 million.

PEOPLE

Vilnius has suffered minimal population loss since the restoration of independence, with a drop of perhaps 10,000 over that period. It is currently around 580,000. This is in contrast to the 10% or more losses faced by Riga and Tallinn over the same period. Whilst some young people are attracted abroad, in the short-term, very few stay for long periods and Vilnius also attracts younger people from the countryside for the inevitable better jobs and prospects that a big city can offer. A little over half of the residents of Vilnius are Lithuanian-speakers; Polish- and Russian-speakers each comprise about 20%.

Lithuanians are often viewed as more self-deprecating than their neighbours, being more concerned with failure than with success but they are also extremely competitive by nature and like to achieve and do better than others. For those brought up on Soviet publications, it is, however, refreshing to see how willing Vilnius City Council is to publicise the difficulties it faces in retaining young people, reducing social differentiation and tackling the inherited stock of crumbling tower blocks.

RELIGION

The turbulent political background to Vilnius throughout the 20th century is reflected in the diversity of religions practised there. Activity was drastically curtailed during the Soviet period, when a Museum of Atheism was established in St Casimir's Church. About a third of the population before the war were Jewish, and the few of them who survived the Holocaust largely left Vilnius early in the Soviet period. The current community of around 5,000 consists mainly of Jews who have emigrated from other parts of the former Soviet Union. Catholicism has always been strong in Vilnius amongst both Polish- and Lithuanian-speakers whereas the Russian-speakers tend to gravitate to the Orthodox Church.

CULTURE AND FESTIVALS

With Vilnius to become Europe's joint 'Capital of Culture' in 2009, it is difficult to see what more can be done in this field than is under way already. It is hard to find a time in the annual calendar when there is not a festival taking place and in contrast to many European capitals, musical activity is particularly diverse during July and August. This is when the St Christopher's Festival takes place, and it has been an annual event since 1995. Music is offered (usually free of charge) not only in obvious venues such as churches, but also in the open air. The casual ambience of the performances is deceptive. Standards are as high as they would be in any more formal surroundings. At other times of year, it may be a jazz festival, early music or films but these simply augment, and never replace, a regular programme of concerts and operas.

Festivals

Vilnius hosts an extremely varied programme of festivals throughout the year. In winter, two stand out – **Užgavėnės**, Lithuania's festive Shrove Tuesday celebrations, when people don hideous masks and strange clothes, play games and light bonfires, and the more accessible **St Casimir's Market**, a huge handicrafts market in the Old Town, which marks the beginning of spring on the first weekend of March. 'Verbos', clusters of dried wild flowers and grasses, are bought to decorate the home. In the last week of May, **Skamba Skamba Kankliai** is a knees-up of lively folk songs, dances and frolics in the Old Town's courtyards and parks, played mostly on traditional Lithuanian instruments. **Rasos**, the pagan midsummer solstice on 23 June, is not as raucous or as wild as it is in neighbouring Latvia, but the celebrations on the banks of the Neris by the White Bridge, and also in the old Lithuanian capital of Kernavė, end only with the coming of the rising sun. Wreaths of grasses are worn and floated on the river, the men leap over fires and at midnight everyone wistfully searches for the magic fern blossom.

The **Day of Statehood** is an open-air display of patriotism on 6 July with a military parade, classical music concert and fireworks.

Then follow two of Vilnius's best festivals, starting with the faultlessly executed **St Christopher Summer Festival**, an exhilarating celebration of organ, chamber and symphony music, usually with some jazz, flamenco and classical guitar music too, arranged by the eponymous chamber orchestra in July and August.

In the first week of September, **Capital Days** is an international city festival extravaganza, one of Vilnius's key multi-art form events of the year. It takes place along Gedimino Avenue, Town Hall Square and Vingis Park. All events are open and free of charge.

Massive sculptures made of straw and filled with fireworks are burned in Kalnų Park during the mystical **Fire Sculptures Festival** on or around 21 September, marking the autumn equinox.

In Trakai, **Three Days Three Nights** is an annual beer festival aimed at cheering everyone up at the end of September with knights' battles and fencing. Finally, **Vilnius Jazz** at the start of October features international jazz, blues, electronic and avant-garde music.

JURGA IVANAUSKAITĖ, VILNIUS'S MYSTICAL NOVELIST

Jurga Ivanauskaitė, a colourful, mysterious, exotic figure in the Vilnius literary landscape, has been at the forefront of Vilnius' new generation of independent-minded novelists and artists for 20 years. Her first books established her reputation as an unconventional writer. The easy style and contemporary characters of her first short stories were an immediate popular success. Making use of her family's unusually rich library – her grandfather was Kostas Korsakas, one of Lithuania's Marxist literary critics – she popularised non-Marxist ideas. Her youthful characters played Beatles songs, enthused about surrealist painters and contemplated the exciting mysticism of Carlos Castaneda. They were misunderstood, frequently depressed and disappointed with life.

Partly, it was her family background that helped her publish her books through Vaga, which until 1990 was the only outlet for fiction in Lithuania. It could also be said that in her favour was the fact that she was regarded as less of a threat by the Soviet authorities because she was female. That a young woman could be a literary rebel was unheard of in both Soviet and pre-Soviet Lithuania. Critics ignored her books, as they did anything they disapproved of.

Jurga Ivanauskaitė's 1993 novel, *Ragana ir lietus* (The Witch and the Rain) caused a national scandal. A love story told by three women – a modern-day bohemian outsider, a medieval witch and Mary Magdalene – it was immediately condemned in official circles as common pornography. But it sold 20,000 copies in two weeks.

In the mid-1990s, Ivanauskaitė's books underwent a complete transformation after she travelled to India and Tibet. Three groundbreaking non-fiction books on Tibetan life and religion were the remarkable result. A collection of traveller's tales and insights into the religion, political situation and everyday reality of Tibetans living in exile in northern India, *Tibet in Exile* has a personal foreword by the Dalai Lama, whom Ivanauskaitė met on several occasions.

In *Journey to Shambhala* the author describes many of her personal experiences and experiments with Buddhism. The book is beautifully illustrated with mandalas, painted at moments of intense inner conflict between her Western background and her new experiences of living and being instructed by lamas in Ladakh and Nepal. *Lost Promised Land* recounts her incredible journey to occupied Tibet. For some time before her departure in June 1998, her name had been on a Chinese blacklist as the leader of a Tibet support group in Lithuania. On reaching the sacred land by 'a secret route via Hong Kong suggested by friends', she discovers the ruinous 'lost promised land' of Tibet.

Jurga Ivanauskaitė is as popular a choice for journalists' interviews as ever. She wears extravagant make-up and Eastern clothes, whether speaking at a meeting of enthusiastic fans or going to her local store in Vilnius to buy groceries.

Lithuania's best-known festival, the **World Lithuanian Song Festival** takes place in the parks of Vilnius every four or five years, the next likely to be in 2008. Thousands of participants come from Lithuanian communities around the world to sing and dance in this spectacular week-long, open-air event. A series of rehearsals is followed by three climactic and colourful performances, the first by song and dance groups together, the second by only dance troupes, and the final breathtaking performance by a 10,000-strong choir at the Song Festival Dome in Vingis Park.

GEOGRAPHY AND CLIMATE

In the summer, Vilnius benefits from a continental climate but in the winter it suffers for it. Between June and August, visitors can usually rely on temperatures between 20°C and 25°C during the day with the occasional really hot day as well. There are a sufficient number of hot days now for the four-star hotels to feel the need to install air conditioning. From November to March temperatures will normally be below freezing point, and quite often a lot below; −10°C is not uncommon, even during the day. Spring and autumn are both short seasons, with erratic changes in temperature, although they should only vary between freezing point and around 15°C.

Planning

THE CITY – A PRACTICAL OVERVIEW

Vilnius is very easy to visit on a short break. Most of the hotels are in the Old Town, or just over the river from it. Within the city, visitors will hardly need to use a bus or taxi as so many of the churches, museums, cafés and clubs are within walking distance of each other. In fact, given the complex one-way traffic systems that operate through most of the Old Town, walking is often much quicker than taking a taxi. Three days is definitely needed to do justice to the major points of interest and many visitors wisely stay longer. Trakai Castle, with its lakeside setting, makes a congenial day trip and Kaunas too offers the same, though its attractions are totally different. Both are easily accessible by public transport. With the multiplicity of flights now serving Vilnius, it is even possible to choose the most convenient time of day for arrival and departure.

Packages booked over a weekend are usually cheaper than mid-week ones as hotels still have more business customers through the year than tourists. Prices for both flights and hotels are higher in the summer months (May–Sep) than at other times of year but even then, by booking well in advance prices can often be much lower than elsewhere in Europe.

Museums open purely for the convenience of the staff rather than for visitors so even in the summer most close all day on Monday and several do not open before 11.00 on other days. Churches open of course for early-morning mass but then stay open all day and often into the evening as well. Shops likely to be of interest to tourists stay open into the evening and kiosks with even longer hours abound throughout the city. Erratic supplies died with the Soviet Union so there is no need to worry about replacing a forgotten toothbrush or obtaining a specific medicine. It is essential to use the local currency in all shops, at least until Lithuania enters the eurozone, but credit cards are accepted everywhere for more expensive purchases and for meals.

WHEN TO VISIT

As Vilnius has so much to offer indoors, the weather matters less here than in towns with more outdoor attractions. The quiet in the narrow lanes criss-crossing the Old Town, the frequent snowfalls and the chance to enjoy the floodlighting are all fair competition during the winter months for the long evenings of daylight, the balmy weather and the outdoor music which are the obvious attractions of summer. January is probably a month to avoid, when the weather is likely to be at its coldest and the colour surrounding Christmas suddenly vanishes. Many visitors do in fact now come just before Christmas, as they can be sure of tasteful and reasonably-priced souvenirs. Some people forget that Vilnius does not sell only amber, although this is an obvious attraction. May and October are perhaps the nicest months for visiting. The spring or autumn colours enhance the parks, prices are low for hotels and flights, while good weather and a full 12 hours of daylight ensure a congenial environment for sightseeing.

SUGGESTED ITINERARIES
Day one

Start with half a day beside the cathedral. A visit here, and then to the National Museum and the Applied Arts Museum, will immediately show how close the town's links have been with cultures to the south rather than with those to the north, above all with the Catholic Church. By 2009, there will be another attraction here, immediately behind the cathedral, and this is the rebuilt royal palace where work started in 2003. Weather permitting, the journey on the funicular railway to the top of the castle will give a view of Vilnius that reflects each of its conquerors and now the planning policies of a totally independent Lithuania. Note Gedimino Avenue which starts at the cathedral and which is now a pedestrian precinct during the evening. Perhaps take lunch on the corner at Literata, no longer a dissident intellectual café, but more a substantial Nordic restaurant.

After lunch, walk along Universiteto to, of course, the university and wander in its courtyards and St John's Church now fully recovered from its 40 years of Soviet desecration. Do not forget to visit its bookshop, Littera. The book selection (in English) is fine but even finer is the artistry on its ceiling. Finish at the Picture Gallery and see how extensively Lithuanian artists were able to travel in the 19th century and also how they portrayed Vilnius itself. Many of the local buildings shown are still perfectly recognisable today.

Be sure to take in an early evening concert, preferably in a church so that the music can be enjoyed in the environment for which it was probably written.

Day two

The KGB Museum probably deserves a half-day to itself, as some time is needed for reflection afterwards. Perhaps it is just as well that it is situated a few hundred yards from anywhere else likely to be of interest. During 2006 it is expanding to exhibit all facets of life during the Soviet era.

Town Hall Square is the base for enjoying several of Vilnius's best-known churches and is also where the Kazys Varnelis House Museum is situated. He is probably Lithuania's most generous benefactor, having returned from his US exile not only with a wide variety of his own paintings but also with an even more valuable collection of maps, first editions, furniture and china. Do not forget to leave the square for a short walk into the former Jewish quarter where each passing year brings further restoration and colour.

Day three

It is time now to be outdoors some more. See why Napoleon fell for St Anne's Church on his hurried forays through Vilnius in 1812. Cross the bubbling River Vilnia into Užupis where the poor have been replaced by the capital's most successful people and also by its most amusing. (1 April is the day to see it at its best.) Read the Užupis constitution nailed to the wall on Paupio Street, then visit some of the 'republic's' little galleries. Finish the morning at the Amber Museum before relaxing over lunch at one of the many tasteful cafés along Pilies.

In the afternoon, walk along the river to St Peter and St Paul, undoubtedly the most flamboyant of all the churches in Vilnius. Return along the other bank to see New Vilnius arising, literally, given the number of skyscrapers either complete or being built.

Day four
It is a pity to leave Vilnius, but a day around the Island Castle In Trakai, or in Kaunas should not be missed. The architecture and the surrounding nature are so totally different, as is the pace of life. History has maintained a stronger grip in both places and it should be enjoyed.

TOUR OPERATORS
In the UK, it is surprising how few of the major city-break operators offer Vilnius, even when Tallinn and Riga have been in their programmes for several years. Perhaps the monopoly held by Lithuanian Airlines for so long was a deterrent and the arrival in 2004–05 of British Airways and airBaltic on the route to London will encourage them to think again. However, the Baltic specialists listed below have all offered short breaks in Vilnius for many years and are fully bonded to protect any money passengers have paid. They will not only have reduced air fares to the area but often also lower hotel prices than those generally available to the public. Their staff will be able to give personal advice on the different hotels available.

The companies listed for the US and Canada of course offer longer programmes in the area.

Baltic specialists
UK

Baltic Adventures 1 Hyde Cl, Harpenden, Herts AL5 4NB; ☎ 01582 462283; f 01582 764339; e info@balticadventures.co.uk; www.balticadventures.co.uk

Baltic Holidays 40 Princess St, Manchester M1 6DE; ☎ 0870 7579233; f 0870 120 2973; e info@balticholidays.com; www.balticholidays.com

Kirker Holidays 4 Waterloo Court, 10 Theed St, London SE1 8ST; ☎ 0870 112 3333; f 0870 066 0628; e travel@kirkerholidays.com; www.kirkerholidays.com

Regent Holidays 15 John St, Bristol BS1 2HR; ☎ 0117 921 1711; f 0117 925 4866; e regent@regent-holidays.co.uk; www.regent-holidays.co.uk

Scantours 73 Mornington St, London NW1 7QE; ☎ 020 7554 3530; f 020 7388 5010; e info@ scantours.co.uk; www.scantoursuk.com

Specialised Tours 4 Copthorne Bank, Copthorne, Crawley, West Sussex RH10 3QX; ☎ 01342 712785; f 01342 717042; e info@specialisedtours.com; www.specialisedtours.com.

Vamos Travel 2 Styles Cl, Leamington Spa, Warwks CV31 1LS; ☎ 0870 7624017; f 0870 7621016; e info@vamostravel.com; www.vamostravel.com

USA

Amest Travel 16 Ocean Parkway #19, New York, NY 11218; ☎ 718 972 2217; f 718 851 4175; e info@amest.com; www.amest.com

Union Tours 245 Fifth Av, New York, NY 10016; ☎ 800 451 9511; f 212 683 9511; www.uniontours.com

Vytis Tours 40–24 235th St, Douglaston, New York, NY 11363; ℩ 718 423 6161;
e tours@vytistours.com; www.vytistours.com

Canada
Valhalla Travel 120 Newkirk Rd, Unit 25, Richmond Hill, Ontario L4C 9S7; ℩ 800 265
0459; f 905 737 0304; e info@valhallatravel.com; www.valhallatravel.com

RED TAPE
Since Lithuania joined the EU in May 2004, entry has been very straightforward for
citizens of all other member states, plus Norway and Switzerland. Only an official
ID or passport is required. Citizens of Australia, Canada, New Zealand and the USA
do not require visas, just a current passport, and this applies to many other
nationalities too. South Africans do still need visas, but a visa for one Baltic country
is valid for the other two as well. Up-to-date information is available on the website
of the Lithuanian Foreign Ministry: www.urm.lt.

Lithuanian embassies overseas
Lithuania maintains the foreign embassies listed below; note that some serve more
than one country. The telephone and fax numbers in brackets give firstly the
country code if calling from abroad (which needs, of course, to be preceded by the
international access number 00). This is followed after a space by the city code.
Email and website addresses are given where available.

Belarus Zacharova 68, 220029 Minsk; ☎ (375 17) 2852 448; f (375 17) 2853 337; e amb.by@urm.lt; www.http://by.urm.lt

Canada 130 Albert St, Suite 204, Ottawa, Ontario K1P 5G4; ☎ (1 613) 567 5458; f (1 613) 567 5315; e amb.ca@urm.lt; lithuanianembassy.ca

Estonia Uus tn 15, Tallinn, EE0100; ☎ (372) 631 4030 or 631 4053; f (372) 641 2013; e amb.ee@urm.lt

Finland Rauhankatu 13a, 00170 Helsinki; ☎ (358 9) 608210; f (358 9) 608220; e amb.fi@urm.lt

France 22 bd de Courcelles, 75017 Paris; ☎ (+33 1) 480 10033; f (+33 1) 480 10331; e infolt@magic.fr; www.amb-lituanie-paris.fr

Germany Charitestrasse 9, 10711 Berlin; ☎ (+49 30) 8906810; f (+49 30) 89068115; e info@botschaft-litauen.de; www.de.urm.lt

Ireland 90 Merrion Bridge Rd, Ballsbridge, Dublin 4; ☎ (+353 1) 668 8292; f (+353) 668 0004; e amb.ie@urm.lt

Israel 8 Shaul Hameleh Bd, Amot Mishpat Bldg, Tel Aviv 64733; ☎ (+972 3) 6958 685; f (+972 3) 6958 691; e amb.il@urm.lt. Also serves South Africa and Cyprus.

Kaliningrad Proletarskaja 133; ☎ (+7 4012) 957688; f (+7 4012) 956838; e kons.Kaliningradas@urm.lt

Latvia Rupniecibus iela 24, LV-1010 Riga; ☎ (+371 2) 321519; f (+371 2) 321589; e lt@apollo.lv

Poland al J Ch Szucha 5, 00-580 Warsaw; ☎ (+48 22) 625 3368; f (+48 22) 625 3440; e amb.pl@urm.lt; www.lietova.pl. Also serves Bulgaria and Romania.

Russia 10 Borisoglebsky per, 121069 Moscow; ☎ (+7 495) 785 8605 or 785 8625; f (+7 495) 785 8600 or 785 8649; e amb.ru@urm.lt. There is also a consulate at Ul Ryleyeva 37, 191123

St Petersburg; ☎ (+7 812) 327 0230; f (+7 812) 327 2615; e kons.st-peterburgas@urm.lt
Ukraine 21 Buslivska, 010901 Kiev; ☎ (+380 44) 2540920; f (+380 44) 2540928;
e amb.ua@urm.lt. Also serves Moldova.
UK 84 Gloucester Pl, London W1U 6AU; ☎ (+44) 20 7486 6401 or 7486 6402; f (+44) 20
7486 6403; e chancery@lithuanianembassy.co.uk; www.amb.urm.lt/jk/. There are honorary
consuls in Wales, Northern Ireland, Worcestershire and Scotland in 2005.
USA 2622 16th St NW, Washington, DC 20009; ☎ (+1 202) 234 5860; f (+1 202) 328 0466;
e amb.us@urm.lt; www.ltembassyus.org. Also serves Mexico. There are consulates in the
following locations: 211 E Ontario, Suite 1500, Chicago, IL 60611; ☎ (+1 312) 397 0382; f (+1
312) 397 0385; 420 Fifth Av, New York, NY 10018; ☎ (+1 212) 354 7840; f (+1 212) 354 7911.

CUSTOMS
British visitors should note that although Lithuania is in the EU, tourists are allowed
to bring back only 200 cigarettes into the UK. The same limit applies for visitors
returning from Poland or the other two Baltic states. For alcohol there is only the
normal stipulation that anything brought back must be for personal consumption
and not for sale.

GETTING THERE AND AWAY
By air
Vilnius International is the biggest of the three international airports in Lithuania,
situated about 7km south of the city centre. Unlike the shiny new airports in Riga

and Tallinn, the arrivals hall in Vilnius is in an old Soviet-era building. Taxis are available directly outside. The newer departures hall is immediately behind, reachable by car up a ramp to the right or on foot through the arrivals hall. A new airport terminal is being constructed that will separate arrivals from non-Schengen countries as soon as Lithuania becomes part of this area, probably by 2008. The arrivals hall contains a small currency exchange bureau, cash machine, kiosk and car rental desks. A limited selection of souvenirs can be found in the departures hall. The airport's cafés and bars are basic but functional.

Vilnius has seen an enormous increase in the number of flights operating there from western Europe. London alone has four flights a day from Gatwick, being served by British Airways, airBaltic and Lithuanian Airlines. Since autumn 2005, Lithuanian Airlines has used the trading name FlyLAL. Whilst there are currently no direct services from other UK cities, CSA via Prague offer connections from Birmingham, Manchester, Stansted and Edinburgh, and KLM via Amsterdam have connections to ten UK airports. SAS via Copenhagen provides links to Birmingham, Manchester and Glasgow. No-frills carrier Ryanair now operates to Kaunas, the Lithuanian airport authorities finally giving in to the terms it demanded. The journey from Kaunas to Vilnius involves a bus journey of 90 minutes or so.

For the first ten years after independence, Lithuanian Airlines had a monopoly on many of the routes that they served. This is now changing and their fares have had to drop to reflect it, both the special fares they give to tour operators and those offered to the public. They are even beginning to work with other carriers so that it is now possible to arrange a tour using their flights to Vilnius and BA from Riga or Estonian Air from Tallinn. Most airlines flying to Vilnius are now cutting down on free food and drink.

Fares fluctuate frequently and early bookers are always rewarded with cheaper fares. Airlines operating to the Baltics much prefer a few empty seats rather than ones filled at an absurdly low price. It is normally cheaper to book flights with a tour operator in conjunction with hotel accommodation than to make these arrangements separately. There is the occasional domestic flight between Vilnius and Palanga but given the success in early 2005 of domestic flights in Latvia, airBaltic may well start more regular domestic services in Lithuania too. A flight of 30 minutes instead of a drive of four hours will appeal to many regular travellers as well as to tourists. In December 2005 Lithuanian Airlines introduced direct flights from Palanga to London.

Travellers from the USA can book through fares with Finnair, Lufthansa and SAS but they may often find it is cheaper to fly first to London or Manchester and then to start their Baltic tour from there. Via London is always the best route for travellers from Australia and New Zealand.

airBaltic fly from Vilnius to Riga and Tallinn and from 2004 seriously reduced the fares so that they now can appeal to tourists as well as to business travellers. Given that the bus takes about nine hours from Vilnius to Tallinn, the flight is a much more congenial option.

By bus

Eurolines have an extensive network of international routes which link Vilnius with Poland and Germany to the west and with Latvia and Estonia to the north. A few buses go to Kaliningrad, Minsk and Moscow. At the time of writing, these still cannot be booked online although their timetables can be checked that way: www.eurolines.lt. Tickets can be booked in advance through travel agents who specialise in the Baltics or in person at the Autobuso Stotis (bus station) which is just across the road from the railway station. Cheaper fares apply for the over-60s, students and for return tickets bought several weeks in advance. In early 2006 the one-way fare from Vilnius to Riga was about £8/US$15 and from Vilnius to Tallinn about £11/US$20. In the summer it is essential to pre-book but in the winter it should normally be possible to buy a ticket on departure.

Domestic tickets are sold at the same bus station and timetables for these can be checked on www.toks.lt. Buses leave at least every half-hour to Kaunas and about hourly to most other towns. As with the international services, it is not usually necessary to book these in advance during the winter but in the summer, particularly at weekends, it is advisable. Comfortable buses leave regularly to larger Lithuanian cities like Klaipėda and Panevėžys.

By train

Trains have been in steady decline since the restoration of independence and few routes are likely to be of interest to foreign visitors except perhaps the suburban service to Paneriai, should visitors wish to see the Holocaust memorial there. There are no services at all to Latvia and Estonia, but a few trains still serve Kaliningrad, Minsk and Warsaw. Domestically there is a limited service to Trakai, Kaunas, Klaipėda and Šiauliai but buses are more frequent. The enormous railway station at Vilnius, which has recently been restored, belies the very limited services that operate from it. However, announcements are made in English, tickets are cheap and the toilets are impeccably clean so perhaps there may still be a future for railways in Lithuania. The Minima supermarket in the basement is useful for travellers from both the railway and bus stations.

HEALTH

Well gone are the days when foreigners convinced each other that for the slightest of ailments it was necessary to flee the country for treatment abroad. Now, however serious an accident or illness, it can always be dealt with in Vilnius. With EU inspectors constantly on the prowl in markets, kitchens and in slaughter-houses, the chances of catching a serious infection are very remote. It is recommended, however, that visitors have up-to-date UK vaccines such as tetanus, diphtheria and polio. Local water is safe to drink but fashion dictates to many local young people that it is cooler to waste money on bottled water. Insect repellent is useful in early autumn, particularly by the lakes in Trakai. From the number of *vaistinės* (chemists) to be seen in every town, it would seem that Lithuania is a nation of hypochondriacs but these shops do at least serve all well-known brands of medicine and several which are on prescription in Britain are available over the counter in Lithuania. However, travellers are advised to bring specific medication that might otherwise require prescriptions. The Gedimino Vaistinė at Gedimino 27, close to the Neringa Hotel, is open 24 hours a day.

Dial 03 for an ambulance.

Travel clinics and health information

A full list of current travel clinic websites worldwide is available on www.istm.org. For other journey preparation information, consult www.tripprep.com. Information about various medications may be found on www.emedicine.com/wild/topiclist.htm.

SAFETY

Vilnius is generally considered to be a very safe place to visit. Tourists who are robbed are usually those who leave seedy side-street bars in a drunken stupor very late at night. There have been the inevitable thefts in markets and on crowded public transport but these can usually be avoided by taking the normal sensible precautions. Passports and other valuables should be left in the hotel where there is either a room safe or a hotel one which guests can use. Otherwise leaving them in a locked suitcase in the room is another possibility. All large bills in shops and restaurants can be paid with credit cards so there is never any need to carry around large quantities of cash.

The 'sink' estates where, perhaps inevitably, the drug culture thrives are fortunately well away from the areas visited by tourists. Women will not feel uncomfortable walking on their own.

WHAT TO TAKE

Travellers in winter must be ready for seriously cold weather. It is therefore important to take thick boots, scarves, gloves and a woollen hat. As all buildings are well heated there is no need for woollen underwear or thick jackets. Cafés, theatres and museums all have ample space for hanging coats and changing shoes. Roads are well swept when snow falls, as are most pavements. Because the city is very compact, and surrounded by low hills, strong winds rarely occur.

An overcoat may be necessary as late as May and as early as September. Never forget an umbrella, as clear skies can quickly cloud over, but of course the reverse is equally true, so do not abandon plans for sightseeing simply because of bad weather which is likely to be very temporary.

The electric current in Lithuania, as in most of continental Europe, is 220 volts AC 50Hz. Plugs are the standard European two-pin variety so it is necessary to take an adaptor from the UK for using hairdryers and to charge mobile phones.

MONEY
Currency

In 1993 Lithuania re-introduced its pre-war currency, the litas (abbreviated throughout this book as Lt), which is divided into 100 centas. This has been the only legal tender within the country ever since. It comes in notes of 10, 20, 50, 100, 200 and 500Lt, while there are coins of 1, 2, 5, 10, 20 and 50 centas and 1, 2 and 5Lt.

On the re-introduction of the currency, the exchange rate was fixed at 4Lt to US$1, and remained pegged at that level until 2002, when it was replaced by a similar fixed link, that of 3.45Lt to € 1. In 2005 the UK pound was therefore worth around 5.00Lt and the US dollar around 2.80Lt. This fixed exchange rate to the euro is scheduled to remain in place until Lithuania formally joins the single European currency, probably in 2008.

Budgeting
Visitors will be pleasantly surprised at how little they need spend in Vilnius without feeling the urge to cut back. Until 2004, this was perhaps appropriate compensation for the high costs of travel and hotels, but with both of these now much lower too, a weekend in Vilnius can in total be cheaper than one much nearer home. With coffee and tea at around 50p/$0.80 a cup and main dishes in many restaurants at less than £5/US$9 throughout the Old Town, there is no need to rush into suburbia to save money. The train or bus fares to Trakai and Kaunas at around £2/US$4 and £3/US$6 respectively are little more than what a single ticket costs within many western European capitals now. The compactness of Vilnius means that tourists rarely need taxis or local buses and again these are both very cheap.

All museums have a charge, which is usually between 50p/$0.90 and £1/US$2 but this is halved for senior citizens and for students. Some museums do not charge on certain days of the week or certain days of the year but it is hardly worth planning an itinerary around these savings!

Kiosks charge roughly the same as shops for day-to-day items so there is no need to queue in the supermarket for toothpaste, bars of chocolate or drinks. Bus tickets should be bought there as they cost 1.10Lt as opposed to 1.40Lt if bought from the driver on the bus itself. Kiosks also sell postcards and English-language publications such as *Vilnius in Your Pocket* and the *Baltic Times*.

Cigarettes are sold at prices not seen in Britain since the early 1970s, about 40p/$0.75 a pack, but do remember that only 200 can be brought back into the UK, despite Lithuania being in the EU. However, there are only the airline weight limits to consider when buying litres of vodka for around £4/US$7 a bottle.

Tipping

Up to 10% is very welcome in restaurants, cafés and hairdressers if the service deserves it, but not otherwise. One or two expensive restaurants now add a service charge to the bill, so in such circumstances remember not to tip twice!

Money

Practicalities

CHANGING MONEY

It is important to insist on receiving low-value notes when changing money as notes of about 20Lt are often difficult to exchange in museums, cafés and kiosks where tourists are likely to spend most of their cash. Lithuanian currency can be ordered from UK banks before departure and is also available at Gatwick airport from where all direct flights to Vilnius left in 2005. Banks throughout Estonia and Latvia, and also those in Poland near to the border, also sell litas. An exchange office, with good rates, is always open at Vilnius airport when flights arrive and the one situated between the bus and railway stations is open 24 hours a day. Those in the town centre tend to keep to office hours, although several do open on Saturdays and Sundays. Unlike in Estonia and Latvia, rates vary very little between the different banks and exchange offices, no matter which currency is exchanged.

The use of credit and debit cards, particularly Visa and MasterCard, has become very widespread in Lithuania during the past few years and it is well worth carrying at least one or both of these. In addition to obtaining cash advances at banks, they can also be used in the many automatic teller machines (ATMs). These are sometimes located within banks, post offices or shops, but many are on the street, offering another 24-hour banking facility. They all offer instructions in five languages, including English. Do however check before leaving home what charges your bank will make for such use. Practices vary enormously and if a charge is made for each transaction, it would be better to use cash. Credit cards are also accepted in all hotels, as well as by many restaurants and shops. A credit card is pretty well mandatory for hiring a car, as most rental companies, and in particular the international ones, insist on payment being made that way.

Travellers' cheques should be avoided; even many banks will not now accept them, seeing them perhaps as a relic of the Soviet Union. Junior staff in banks will probably not even know what they are.

LOCAL MEDIA

Visitors interested in recent political news from the Baltic area should buy the *Baltic Times* which is published in Riga every Thursday and is usually on sale in Vilnius the same afternoon. It also lists concerts and films for the next week. *Vilnius Monthly* started publication only in 2005, but it has quickly made its mark amongst the expat community. However, its articles on culture and history lack context and are really only for those who live in Vilnius. *VilniusNOW!* also started publication in 2005, following the success of a similar monthly magazine in Riga. It is distributed in hotels and concentrates on dining and entertainment. It also has informative business features. The opening of an office for it in Vilnius should ensure that all major hotels will stock copies.

The bi-monthly *Vilnius in Your Pocket* has built up for itself a legendary status since it started in 1992; it became immediately notorious for the sharpness of its pen in the face of bland service, unimaginative décor and tepid food. As standards have improved so much since then, it can usually adopt a more positive tone, but it remains as harsh as ever about the places that still deserve it.

Travellers also planning to visit Riga or Tallinn should try to find the bi-monthly *City Paper*. Its reviews of hotels and restaurants are detailed and in a part of the world not known for lively political and artistic writing, it provides the perfect one-stop shop for English-speaking readers wanting an instant briefing on all the major local issues and attractions.

A few copies of the European editions of British and American daily newspapers are on sale in hotels that cater for business travellers but visitors should not rely on this. No local daily newspaper appears in English nor do local TV stations transmit in English but hotel televisions can nearly always receive BBC World and CNN.

COMMUNICATIONS
Telephone

To reach a landline within Vilnius, just dial the seven-digit number. If phoning from elsewhere in Lithuania, use first the prefix 8 which is used for all out-of-town numbers and then the Vilnius code 5 before the seven-digit number. All mobile numbers have nine digits and these are prefixed with 8, wherever the call is made. Phoning Lithuania from abroad, remember the country prefix of 370 which is followed by the city code and then the local number. For mobiles, the 370 country prefix is followed by 8.

Costs for phone calls made from hotel rooms vary enormously. Some hotels have deliberately reduced their charges to try to persuade guests not to use their mobiles.

Others have left them at the absurdly high rates of the 1990s. Phone boxes take only cards which can be bought at any kiosk. They are issued in sums of 9Lt, 13Lt and 30Lt. Expect to pay about 2Lt a minute to phone Britain or the USA from these boxes, which are increasingly rare in Vilnius as mobiles take over the communications market.

Mobile phone users wanting to avoid roaming costs can of course buy a SIM card for use within their phone. Prices change in this field all the time but local calls should cost only the equivalent of a few pence and international ones about 40p/$0.75 a minute, so similar to the charges payable in a public phone box.

Useful telephone numbers
Fire 01
Police 02
Ambulance 03
Directory enquiries 118
International calls 1573

Post
The main post office is at Gedimino 7 [1 D/E 2] and is open 07.00–19.00 Mon–Fri and 09.00–16.00 on Sat. It sells a wide range of postcards and packing materials for those who need to send parcels. It also sells sets of all the stamps that have been issued in Lithuania since the re-establishment of independence in 1991. Its website www.post.lt gives full information on current tariffs.

Internet

At the time of writing only two hotels, the Artis and the Centrum Uniquestay, provided computers free of charge in each room. Most others provide connections for those who wish to use their laptops but do check charges before settling down to a few hours of emailing. Some provide computers in a business centre for guests, which may be free of charge (as at the Novotel) or may have a cost. With WIFI spreading so quickly, it is impossible to give up-to-date guidance for reception, except to say that all hotels with conference facilities are bound to have it. To check the current situation, refer to www.wifi.lt.

There are not many Internet cafés in Vilnius, perhaps because so many local people can now afford to have computers at home, or the use of them in their offices. As the Reval Hotel Lietuva charges 20Lt an hour for its computers, some guests walk across the river to the Old Town where Collegium at Pilies 22 offers congenial surroundings and Internet access for 8Lt an hour. Unlike the city's other Internet cafés, there might even be people as old as 25 working there. It opens at 08.00 and closes at 24.00.

EMBASSIES IN VILNIUS

The number of foreign embassies in Vilnius increases every year, as more countries feel the need for direct representation there rather than treating Lithuania as a sideline from an embassy in Riga, Stockholm or Warsaw. The website of the Lithuanian Foreign Ministry (*www.urm.lt*) gives a full list together with all contact details. The main ones likely to be of interest to readers of this book are listed below. Whilst the phone numbers given will probably be answered in office hours only, there will be a recorded message at other times with the mobile phone number of the duty officer should urgent contact be needed.

Belarus Mindaugo 13; ✆ (5) 266 2200; f (5) 266 2212; e lithuania@belembassy.org; www.belarus.lt

Canada Jogailos 4; ✆ (5) 249 0950; f (5) 249 7865; e vilnius@canada.lt; www.canada.lt

France Švarco 1; ✆ (5) 212 2979; f (5) 212 4211; e ambafrance.vilnius@diplomatie.gouv.fr; www.ambafrance-lit.org

Russia Latvių 53/54; ✆ (5) 272 1763; f (5) 272 3877; e rusemb@rusemb.lt; www.lithuania.mid.ru

UK Antakalnio 2; ✆ (5) 246 2900; f (5) 246 2901; e be-vilnius@britain.lt; www.britain.lt

USA Akmenų 6; ✆ (5) 266 5500; f (5) 266 5510; e mail@usembassy.lt; www.usembassy.lt

HOSPITALS AND PHARMACIES

You can find a pharmacy (*vaistinė*) on virtually every street in Vilnius, but only one is open 24 hours: **Gedimino Vaistinė** (*Gedimino 27;* ✆ *(5) 261 0135*). Professional medical care that reaches the sort of standards found in private hospitals in Western countries is available at two locations. If you have private health insurance in your home country you may be exempt from payment, so if possible ask about this beforehand.

Baltic-American Medical & Surgical Clinic, Nemenčinės pl 54a; \ (5) 234 2020; f (5) 276 79 42; e bak@takas.lt; www.bak.lt

Medical Diagnostic Centre, Grybo 32/10; \ (5) 270 9120; f (5) 270 9127; e mdc@medcentras.lt; www.medcentras.lt

Professional medical check-ups in English are also provided by appointment at a small clinic right next door to the cathedral: **Medicine General Private Clinic**, Gedimino 1a (2nd floor); \ (5) 261 3534; f (8) 684 33100; e medgen@takas.lt; www.clinic.lt. *Open Mon-Fri, 09.00–17.00.*

ENGLISH-LANGUAGE CHURCH SERVICES
Grace International Baptist Church Verkių 22; www.church.lt. Services every Sun at 11.00.

International Church of Vilnius Vokiečių 20; www.icvilnius.org. An ecumenical service is held in the Lutheran church every Sun at 09.30.

SS Philip and James Lukiškių aikštė 10; Roman Catholic mass every Sun at 09.00 with confessions beforehand on request.

TOURIST INFORMATION
There are two offices in the Old Town (at Vilniaus 22 [1 D3] and at Didžioji 31 [4 F5]) and one at the railway station which therefore also serves the bus station, as they are side by side. There isn't one at the airport. Although they are called

'Municipal Tourist Offices' all three can also provide information on other places in Lithuania. The one with the address in Didžioji is in fact in the Old Town Hall in the centre of the Square.

Opening hours vary on a seasonal basis but they are all open at weekends during the summer and sometimes on Saturdays during the winter. Minimum hours at all offices during the week in winter are 10.00–17.00. ℩ (5) 262 9660; e tic@vilnius.lt; www.turizmas.vilnius.lt.

MAPS

City guides such as *Vilnius In Your Pocket* and *VilniusNOW!* have detailed street plans of the city centre. Telephone directories have maps that go beyond, into the suburbs. There is an excellent series of maps on Vilnius and other cities in the Baltic region by the Latvian publisher **Jana Seta** (*www.kartes.lv*). These are updated every year and are available in Britain at Stanfords in London, Manchester and Bristol. They are also available in bookshops and petrol stations in Vilnius, as are maps by the Lithuanian publisher **Briedis** (*www.briedis.lt*). An interactive map and street plan of the whole of Lithuania can be found at www.maps.lt.

LOCAL TOUR OPERATORS

The following travel agencies can organise bus/walking/cycling tours of Vilnius, Lithuania and the Baltic states:

Local tour operators

Krantas Pylimo 4; ☏ (5) 231 3314; f (5) 262 9120; e vilnius@vilnius.krantas.lt;
www.krantas.lt
Lithuanian Holidays Šeimyniškų 4; ☏ (5) 272 4154; f (5) 272 1815;
e contact@lithuaniantour.com; www.lithuaniantours.com
Lithuanian Tours Šeimyniškių str 18, ☏ (5) 272 4154; f (5) 272 1815;
e contact@lithuaniantours.com; www.lithuaniantours.com
Liturimex Basanavičiaus 11; ☏ (5) 279 1416; f (5) 279 1417; e center@liturimex.lt;
www.liturimex.lt

Practicalities

Local transport

4

AIRPORT TRANSFER

Two buses and several minibuses operate from the airport into town. Bus tickets should be bought on arrival from the kiosk at the airport where they cost 1.10Lt, or 1.40Lt if bought from the driver. The number 1 runs to the bus/train station [3 E8]/[4 F8] and the number 2 runs along Švitrigailos across Gedimino and then crosses the river to the Lietuva and Holiday Inn hotels. Unfortunately no buses pass any of the hotels in the Old Town but none are more than a few hundred yards from a bus stop.

Microbuses operate along these routes as well and also on others. They usually charge 2.00Lt and payment is always made to the driver. They stop at all bus stops but will also stop elsewhere. They do not operate within the Old Town. Services by both means of transport operate from early in the morning until fairly late at night so there is almost always public transport, no matter when a flight leaves or arrives.

BUSES AND TROLLEYBUSES

There are a wide number of routes except into the Old Town, where only one bus, the number 11, operates and that only on a half-hourly basis. However a bus stop is never far away wherever you are in the Old Town. Some bus stops have maps showing all the routes and all buses have the main streets along which they travel marked on a side window. Stotis is the railway/bus station where many routes start and finish. Tickets cost 1.10Lt if bought in a kiosk and 1.40Lt if bought from the driver on the bus. In either case, remember to punch them at the start of your journey. There is no reducton for buying a larger quantity as there is in Tallinn.

Full timetables and routes are given on www.vilnius.transport.lt. Much of the fleet, it has to be admitted, is quite elderly but since 2004 serious efforts have been made to replace the entire rolling stock so travellers should be sure of a comfortable ride on many routes.

CAR HIRE

There is no point in hiring a car within Vilnius but there are several places on the outskirts of the town for which it would be useful, such as the Television Tower, Europe Park and the Antakalnis Cemetery. It could also be useful for visiting Kaunas and Trakai where some of the sites are a distance from public transport. In the summer, cars are often booked well in advance so this should be arranged through travel agents abroad at the same time as hotels and flights are booked. However, the firms listed below may be able to help at short notice. Apart from Aunela, they all have offices at the airport and can deliver cars there or to a hotel in town.

Aunela ⟩ (8) 686 63444; e aunela@takas.lt; www.aunela.lt
Avis ⟩/f (5) 232 9316; e apo@avis.lt; www.avis.lt
Budget ⟩ (5) 230 6708; f (5) 230 6709; e budget@budget.lt; www.budget.lt
Hertz ⟩ (5) 272 6940; f (5) 272 6970 e hertz@hertz.lt; www.hertz.lt
Litinterp ⟩ (5) 212 3850; f (5) 212 3559; e vilnius@litinterp.com
Sixt ⟩ (5) 239 5636; f (5) 239 5635; e rent@sixt.lt; www.sixt.lt

TAXIS

Vilnius taxi drivers had a very bad reputation amongst foreigners in the early '90s, but now problems are few and far between. As anywhere else, enter only a clearly marked car, and check that the meter is turned on immediately. On this basis a journey within the city should not cost more than about £2/US$4 and one to the airport about £4/US$8. At the airport, charges are clearly marked in English on a board beside the taxi rank outside the terminal.

Taxis ordered by phone are a little cheaper than those hailed on the street so if you can get a Lithuanian speaker to do this, take advantage of it. Tip 10% if the driver is polite, does not smoke and turns the radio off when you enter. Reputable companies of several years' standing include:

Denvila ↘ (5) 244 4444
Ekipažas ↘ (5) 239 5540
Martonas ↘ (5) 240 0004
Vilniaus ↘ (5) 212 8888

CYCLING

The streets of Vilnius are a little more cyclist-friendly than other eastern European cities, but drivers can be aggressive and impatient, especially at peak hours. So nobody's going to stop you if you cycle your velocipede on the pavements.

In summer 2001, Mayor Artūras Zuokas introduced 1,000 distinctive orange bikes to Vilnius for public use. Cycle paths were painted and metal racks installed at strategic points throughout the city centre, the idea being that you could jump on a bike and cycle to your chosen destination for free, leaving the bicycle at the nearest rack. Needless to say, every single bike was stolen within hours. But the cycle paths still exist, making pedalling through the Old Town a pleasurable experience.

You can rent a bicycle, and also find out more about biking through the Baltics, at:

Lithuanian Cyclists Community, PO Box 61, LT 01002 Vilnius; ℩ (8) 699 56009; f (5) 278 4330; e BaltiCCycle@bicycle.lt; www.bicycle.lt

Accommodation

5

There is a wide choice of accommodation in Vilnius, ranging from dorm beds in hostels to luxury hotels. Prices are similarly variable, and are usually a fairly reliable indicator of the quality of any particular establishment.

The years 2003–04 saw a sudden burst of activity in hotel construction, with about 20 new locations opening in that short space of time, in a wide variety of locations and catering to an equally wide variety of clientele. The de-luxe traveller can now rely on the chains that prevail elsewhere, whilst budget travellers are no longer dependent on a haphazard range of guesthouses. There will be further increases in 2007; amongst other hotels due to open then is a Kempinski opposite the cathedral. Many tourists automatically choose the Old Town but regular visitors to Vilnius are now increasingly turning to the larger hotels over the river and in the New Town where rooms are bigger, views more extensive and driving less problematical. Short periods of intense heat in the summers of 2002 and 2003 persuaded most hotels in the four- and five-star category to install air conditioning, even though it only needs to be used for about four to five weeks in most years. Because supply nearly always exceeds demand in Vilnius (unlike in Riga and Tallinn) hotel prices are reasonable on a year-round basis and many agents can offer considerable reductions on the rates advertised by the hotels directly. The published rates are those quoted in the listings.

Independent travellers, however, are unlikely to be offered discounts in summer, even if they stay for several nights, but do ask about weekend rates, which some hotels provide. Prices are generally lower in winter, when you are likely to find a room in most hotels just by turning up on the day. In summer, independent travellers are advised to book ahead. Breakfast is frequently included in the price.

Accommodation is available at the airport but it is not of high quality and as the drive from town takes only 20 minutes by bus and 15 minutes by car, there is no need to use it. Hotels at the airport have therefore not been included here. There are rumours of improvements taking place in 2006 so perhaps such hotels can feature in the next edition of the book.

LUXURY HOTELS

All the hotels listed in this section are the recipients of an official five-star rating from the Lithuanian State Department of Tourism, or should be due for one.

Crowne Plaza Čiurlionio 84; ✆ (5) 274 3400; f (5) 274 3411; e reservation@cpvilnius.com; www.cpvilnius.com [*Vilnius* map]
This huge tower block is a longish walk from the Old Town, though it profits from a pleasantly leafy location at the edge of Vingis Park. It is one of the very few hotels that functioned in communist times, but it was completely rebuilt in 2003; all the bedrooms are now equipped to state-of-the-art business and conference standards. In the basement are a swimming pool, sauna and gym. Fine views over the city can be enjoyed from the 16th floor Horizon bar, while the restaurant, The Seasons, presents an international menu, including a choice of vegetarian dishes. *Sgls 304–342Lt, dbls 304–376Lt, suites 328–532Lt, apartments 449–656Lt.*

Grotthuss Ligoninės 7; ✆ (5) 266 0322; f (5) 266 0323; e info@grotthusshotel.com; www.grotthusshotel.com [3 E6]

The hotel advertises that it is a 5-min walk from the President's Office, which suggests the sort of clientele to which it aims to appeal. Although situated on a small street in the Old Town, the rooms are all large enough to work in and the choice of flowers and pictures that abound make work here much more congenial than it otherwise might be. Hopefully its neighbours around the rear courtyard gradually adopt its aesthetic sense as well. An atrium in this courtyard is the location for its well-known restaurant La Pergola. Exclusivity here is ensured by restricting the number of tables to five, but somehow the dishes on its extensive menu always seem to be available. *Sgls 420Lt, dbls 550Lt, suites 700Lt.*

Kempinski Hotel AAA e info.project.vilnius@kempinski.com [2 F4]

Due to open in 2007, the 107-room Kempinski will be on the edge of the Old Town directly facing the castle, cathedral and bell tower. The 19th-century façade of this former telegraph building is being preserved while the interior will be renovated to offer elegant facilities, such as international restaurants, business centre and health club. Two extension wings are being built.

Le Meridien Villon A2 highway; ✆ (5) 273 9700; f (5) 273 9730; e info@lemeridien.lt; www.lemeridien.lt

This is a huge motel and conference centre, located 19km from the centre of Vilnius, beside the main highway to Panevėžys and Riga. It lays on free shuttle buses to the city, and offers the services of a full holiday complex, including tennis courts, a fitness club, swimming pool and 3 saunas. Despite its distance from town the restaurant, Le Paysage, specialising in Gallic-influenced cuisine has such a reputation that many people are happy to make the journey. *Sgls 550–690Lt, dbls 600–730Lt, suites 1,000Lt, apartments 2,900Lt.*

Narutis Pilies 24; ℡ (5) 212 2894; f (5) 262 2882; e info@narutis.com; www.narutis.com [2 G3]

With tasteful French furniture and even frescoes in some of the rooms, the elegant Narutis is set in a 16th-century building on the Old Town's partly pedestrianised main street. Guests reach their rooms from a central plush lounge with its own glass elevator. Ask for the upper floors where the views of the Pilies Street market are best. The cosy Kristupo Café serves excellent food on the ground floor and dining is available in an atmospheric vaulted cellar. Now a member of the Summit Hotels & Resorts chain, the Narutis retains its own unique charm. *Sgls 450Lt, dbls 600–800Lt, suites 900Lt.*

Radisson SAS Astorija Didžioji 35/2; ℡ (5) 212 0110; f (5) 212 1762; e reservations.vilnius@radissonsas.com; www.radissonsas.com [4 F5/6]

This grand early 20th-century hotel in the heart of the Old Town has been refurbished by the Radisson SAS chain, and has a recently opened (2004) health centre prominent among its facilities. All rooms have hairdryer, trouser press, telephone, cable TV, safe. Business-class rooms are larger, have tea/coffee/kettle in them and guests have free access to the health centre. A 'grab and run' breakfast is available in the lobby, but it is a great pity to take it when the alternative is to enjoy a leisurely and lavish buffet breakfast overlooking part of Town Hall Square. *Sgls 550Lt, dbls 580Lt, suite 1,725Lt.*

Stikliai Gaono 7; ☏ (5) 264 9595; f (5) 212 3870; e sales@stikliaihotel.lt; www.stikliaihotel.lt [2 F4]

At an unbeatable location on a narrow cobblestone street in the Old Town, the richly decorated, 5-star Stikliai has stubbornly held on to its reputation as the city's most exclusive hotel since it opened shortly before Lithuania's independence. Royals and celebrities from Western Europe have slept in its four-poster beds, reclined on its sofas and dined in the restaurant on expensive French cuisine. They may also have used its sauna, swimming pool and fitness room. *Sgls 570–775Lt, dbls 690–775Lt, suites 890–1,240Lt, apartments 3,800Lt.*

FIRST-CLASS HOTELS

The hotels in this section have all been allocated a four-star rating.

Art Hotel Pilies 34 ☏ (5) 266 1626; f (5) 266 1627 [2 G4]

At the time of writing in early 2006, this hotel was closed for a complete refurbishment. All the rooms except for one suite will be named after artists whose works will adorn the walls. The paintings will apparently not be mere reproductions; they will be 'near-originals'. Most artists will be impressionists, but guests with an earlier taste can go for the Leonardo room. Those not bothered with privacy will presumably take the suite, called Nude, which has a balcony over Pilies, one of the busiest streets in the Old Town. *Sgls 350Lt, dbls 420Lt.*

Artis Liejykos 11/23; ☏ (5) 266 0363 or 266 0366; f (5) 266 0377; e artis@centrum.lt; www.centrum.lt [1 E4]

The latest addition to Vilnius's Centrum group of hotels occupies a refurbished Old Town mansion overlooking the President's Office garden, so in a very quiet location. All twin/double rooms have baths and fabric paintings on the walls. Singles are on the small side here and have conventional paintings. A recent expansion has seen the opening of a swimming pool and gym to which hotel guests have access free of charge. The restaurant is very reasonably priced for a hotel of this standard. *Sgls 430Lt, dbls 500Lt, suites 690Lt.*

Atrium Pilies 10; ☎ (5) 210 7773; f (5) 210 7770; e hotel@atrim.lt; www.atrium.lt [2 G3]
Situated in a peaceful courtyard just off one of the busiest streets in the heart of the Old Town, this hotel boasts large and well-appointed bedrooms. It has an excellent Argentinian restaurant, El Gaucho, which naturally specialises in steaks. *Sgls 300–550Lt, dbls 390–550Lt, suites 700–800Lt.*

Barbacan Palace Bokšto 19; ☎ (5) 266 0840; f (5) 266 0841; e barbacan@centrokubas.lt; www.centrokubas.lt [4 G5]
The hotel is under the same management as the Centro Kubas listed below but they could not be more different. The Barbacan is larger, and is one of the many hotels that opened in 2003. It has conventional décor throughout and is on a quiet side street at the edge of the Old Town. Many rooms have a view of the Artillery Bastion and the restaurant/café has prices well below those normally to be expected in the Old Town. Its original features are a basement bowling alley and billiards table, with reduced prices for hotel guests. *Sgls 360Lt, dbls 385Lt, suites 450Lt.*

Accommodation

Best Western Naujasis Vilnius Konstitucijos 14; ☏ (5) 273 9595; f (5) 273 9500;
e office@hotelnv.lt; www.hotelnv.lt [*Vilnius* map]
With 114 rooms, this hotel used to be considered large but, with the refurbished Reval
Lietuva now towering over it, suddenly it seems small. Every two years it is updated so
perhaps is typical of any go-ahead Lithuanian organisation. Finally the surroundings are
getting updated too, so there is no need to flee into the Old Town for shopping or different
restaurants. Soon it should be an integral part of 'business Vilnius' which is taking over this
side of the river. *Sgls 340Lt, dbls 400Lt, suites 500–560Lt, apartments 600–66Lt.*

Centro Kubas Stiklių 3; ☏ (5) 266 0860; f (5) 266 0863; e hotel@centrokubas.lt;
www.centrokubas.lt [2 F4]
A designer-style hotel decked out with old agricultural tools in all the public areas and in
the rooms too. A windmill dominates the lobby. There are only 14 rooms, spread across
four floors and linked by a glass lift. A peephole in each room is part of the security
arrangements. Use of laptop computers is free of charge. *Sgls 320Lt, dbls 360Lt.*

Centrum Uniquestay Vytenio 9/24; ☏ (5) 268 3300; f (5) 213 2760; e hotel@centrum.lt;
www.uniquestay.com [*Vilnius* map]
The Tallinn-based, British-run Uniquestay group took over the management of this hotel in
2003, so computers were placed in every room at once, as were tea- and coffee-making
facilities. Being a 10-min walk from the Old Town, it has taken advantage of the location to
offer enormous space in the public areas and larger rooms than might otherwise be
expected. Most of these therefore have baths, and not just showers. It used to be seen as

First-class hotels

purely a business hotel, but has recently been successful in attracting tourists. The 4th floor has cheaper, smaller rooms with showers only. Easy parking for coaches and cars obviously helps access and departures. The location beside the Belarus Embassy ensures peace and quiet around the clock. *Sgls 265–340Lt, dbls 390Lt, suites 490Lt.*

CityPark Stuokos-Gucevičiaus 3; ☎ (5) 212 3515; f (5) 210 7460; e citypark@citypark.lt; www.citypark.lt [1 E2]

Architectural controversy surrounded the unabashedly modern extension added to the original hotel located in a refurbished building with a central courtyard diagonally opposite the cathedral. The fountains and gardens that were added in front of the hotel in 2004 have made its situation particularly attractive, and this has increased the popularity of its Italian restaurant, Rossini. There is also the rare facility of its own underground car park. *Sgls 360–390Lt, dbls 480–560Lt, suites 660–700Lt.*

Congress Vilniaus 2/15; ☎ (5) 269 1919; f (5) 251 4280; e info@congress.lt; www.congress.lt

Housed in a fine old building overlooking the River Neris, this used to be a budget hotel, but it has been totally refurbished to business-class standards and given a new name so has gone through a similar metamorphosis to the Grand in Tallinn. The name perhaps puts off tourists, which is a pity given its convenient location, but this greatly reduces prices at the weekend. Car-parking and Internet connections are free of charge. *Sgls 300Lt, dbls 400–440Lt, suites 560Lt.*

Conti Raugyklos 7/2; ☎ (5) 251 4111; f 251 4100; e info@contihotel.lt; www.contihotel.lt [3 D6]

The opening of this hotel in 2003 marked the beginning of the regeneration of the rundown area to the rear of the synagogue. It incorporates a host of modern design features including full disabled access, a welcoming lobby with waterfall and well-appointed bedrooms with en-suite facilities and Internet access. All bedrooms have prints showing Vilnius as it was about 100 years ago. Try to get rooms 506, 507 or 508 for the best views of contemporary Vilnius. The kitchens are equipped to allow Jewish groups to prepare kosher food. *Sgls 350Lt, dbls 530Lt.*

Dvaras Manor House Tilto 3; ↘ (5) 210 7370; f (5) 261 8783; e hotel@dvaras.lt; www.dvaras.lt [1 E2]
This is a very select hotel, with just 8 bedrooms, and as its name and its décor suggest, it is eager to promote its grand background. All rooms have AC, and Internet access free of charge. There is a similarly classy restaurant, which serves a wide international menu and has a notable wine list. *Sgls 340Lt, dbls 400Lt.*

Europa Royale Aušros Vartų 6; ↘ (5) 266 0770; f (5) 261 2000; e reservation@hoteleuropa.lt; www.hoteleuropa.lt [4 G6]
A stylish, modern, luxury hotel in a beautifully renovated Old Town building. Heated bathroom tiles are a novelty in the en suites and most have baths rather than just showers. The nicest rooms are on the 4th floor as they have a view over the Gates of Dawn as well as over the Old Town. *Sgls 432–570Lt, dbls 518–656Lt, apartments 760–1,381Lt.*

Grybas House Aušros Vartų 3a; ↘ (5) 261 9695 or 264 7474; f (5) 212 2416; e info@grybashouse.com; www.grybashouse.com [4 G6]
A delightful small hotel (there are only 9 rooms) in a refurbished Baroque house set in a quiet courtyard at the northern end of the Old Town. The décor includes sculptures from

the Congo and the former pier in Palanga. Water filters in every room and heated floors are what all guests remember here, and the gratis airport transfer is a nice gesture too. The Grybas family have run this hotel since it opened in 1992, but have modernised it twice since then. There is a fine basement restaurant, with live classical music on Wed evenings. *Sgls 280Lt, dbls 295Lt, suites 330Lt.*

Holiday Inn Šeimyniškių 1; ℡ (5) 210 3000; f (5) 210 3001; e holiday-inn@ibc.lt; www.holidayinnvilnius.lt

Surprisingly, it took until 2002 for this well-known chain to open a hotel in Vilnius, its first venture into the Baltic states and in 2005 this was still its only property in the region. The location, immediately east of the new business district, was a gamble when they first arrived but it has certainly now paid off. Novel then were baths, AC and proper soundproofing in every room and competitors are now trying to catch up. The easy walk over the river to the Old Town ensures that when business clients leave for the weekend or for the summer, tourists always replace them. *Sgls 420-470Lt, dbls 483–587Lt, suites 656–760Lt, apartments 967Lt.*

Mabre Residence Maironio 13; ℡ (5) 212 2087 or 212 2195; f (5) 212 2240; e mabre@mabre.lt; www.mabre.lt [2 H4]

Occupies the grand neo-classical courtyard buildings of a former Russian Orthodox monastery in the quiet eastern part of the Old Town. High walls give it a very exclusive feel, perhaps rather necessary as it is so close to many of the tourist sites, such as St Anne's Church. Facilities for guests include a sauna and fitness centre and a small pool. There is no charge for Internet access in the rooms. The hotel is well known to Vilnius residents for its

Steakhouse Hazienda, one of the first to open and still one of the best known.
Sgls 320–380Lt, dbls 460–520Lt, suites 580–640Lt, apartments 780–880Lt.

Mano Liza Ligoninės 5; ↘ (5) 212 2225; f (5) 212 2608; e hotel@aaa.lt;
www.hotelinvilnius.lt [3 E6]
This hotel is next door to the grander Grotthuss and both share a passion for good art,
but in other respects the Mano Liza is rather simpler, having only 8 rooms and many guests
are regulars from the USA. *Sgls 280Lt, dbls 300Lt, suites 360Lt, apartments 470Lt.*

Novotel Gedimino 16; ↘ 266 6200; f 266 6201; e H5209@accor.com; www.novotel.com
[1 D2]
This tall hotel became so popular amongst tourists and business visitors as soon as it
opened in 2003 that it is hard to believe that it has not always been part of the post-
independence scene. It has had its fair (perhaps unfair) share of local critics who feel that
such a tall new building has no place so near to the Old Town and that it should have been
built on the other side of the river. Gedimino now being a pedestrian precinct for much of
the day has made a formerly busy location a quieter one, despite all the attractions and
offices nearby. All rooms have baths and these are so placed that the TV can be watched at
the same time. The rooms also have separate showers and all provide tea/coffee-making
facilities. As the gym is on the 7th floor, it is possible to keep fit here with a view. Even
though the restaurant is on the second floor, the view of the activity on Gedimino makes it
an attractive location and its prices have been set to bring in local custom as well as hotel
guests. Its choice of fish dishes is unusual for Vilnius and puts many restaurants in ports to

First-class hotels

shame. The hotel stresses its family orientation, organising amongst other things a supervised Sun brunch and offering a children's menu in the restaurant. *Sgls 350–450Lt, apartments 620Lt.*

Ramada Subačiaus 2; ☎ 255 3355; f (5) 255 3311; e hotel@ramadavilnius.lt; www.ramadavilnius.lt [4 G6]
Emerging late in 2005, the Ramada was the first hotel to open its doors in Vilnius in two years. It is comfortable enough, with the unusual feature of TVs and DVD players in each of the rooms. It benefits from an Old Town location close to the Lithuanian Philharmonic – ask for a room at the front for a busy view, or the back if you want to sleep. There's wireless Internet access in the lobby, but not in the rooms, which tend to be fairly small. No parking available. Lower prices are available for weekend stays. *Sgls 280–330Lt, dbls 350–410Lt, suites 410–790Lt.*

Ratonda Gedimino 52/1; ☎ (5) 212 0670; f (5) 212 0669; e ratonda@centrum.lt; www.centrumhotels.com [*Vilnius* map]
This hotel is under the same management, the Centrum Company, which runs the Artis Hotel. It is not as grand, and the rooms are smaller, but it is convenient for Parliament and government ministries situated near to it. The use of glass in the roof and walls was very special in the mid-1990s when the hotel opened, although is more common now. A sauna and fitness centre were added early in 2005. *Sgls 295–360Lt, dbls 390Lt, suites 490Lt.*

Reval Hotel Lietuva Konstitucijos 20; ☎ (5) 272 6200; f (5) 272 6210; e lietuva.sales@revalhotels.com; www.revalhotels.com [*Vilnius* map]
The former Intourist hotel is much the largest and most prominent in Vilnius, with nearly

300 rooms, and is now the main conference centre in the city. It is quite common in winter for conference guests never to leave the building from one day to the next. In 2000 the hotel was acquired by the Reval chain, which eliminated all Soviet features in a radical Scandinavian-style makeover. The even-numbered rooms offer grandstand views over the Old Town, as does the bar on the 22nd floor, which is at its best around sunset. The number 2 bus from the airport passes the entrance and a pedestrian bridge is the best way to get to the Old Town over the river. The Reval chain runs the equally large Latvia Hotel in Riga, the Ridzene there, four hotels in Tallinn and a hotel in Kaunas due in 2007. More hotels will probably follow. Travel agents can often obtain lower rates if clients book more than one Reval hotel on the same tour. *Sgls 380Lt, dbls 450–625Lt, suites 790Lt, apartments 1,210Lt.*

Šarūnas Raitininkų 4; ☎ (5) 272 3666 or 724888; f (5) 724355; e info@hotelsarunas.lt; www.hotelsarunas.lt [*Vilnius* map]
Not Vilnius's best-located hotel, a good 20-minute walk from the Old Town past a football stadium, the Šarūnas is nevertheless a stylish, modern business hotel owned by NBA basketball star and local hero Šarūnas Marčiulionis. Airport transfer and 24-hour laundry are among the services, together with a well-equipped fitness room and sauna. *Sgls 280–320Lt, dbls 300–340Lt, suites 410–450Lt, apartments 480–600Lt.*

Scandic Neringa Gedimino 23; ☎ (5) 268 1910; f (5) 261 4160; e neringa@scandic-hotels.com; www.scandic-hotels.com [1 C1]
Certainly the most pleasant of the Baltic countries' Scandic hotels, the Neringa benefited from a Scandinavian-style facelift that now perfectly complements Gedimino Avenue's recent overall

First-class hotels

makeover. Two original features stand out: firstly the library with its deep sofas and armchairs and current editions of foreign newspapers and magazines, and secondly the alcoves on every floor that overlook Gedimino, each with armchairs and fresh flowers. The ground-floor Neringa restaurant, which used to hum with the city's artistic elite in the late Soviet years, is worth visiting for its bizarre Socialist Realist murals, though these days the pizza restaurant next door is far more popular. *Sgls 500–600Lt, dbls 700–860Lt, suites 920–1,000Lt.*

Shakespeare Bernardinų 8/8; ↘ (5) 266 5885; f (5) 266 5886; e info@shakespeare.lt; www.shakespeare.lt [2 G3]

This English-style country hotel on an Old Town back street adopts a literary theme, with most of the rooms named after famous writers and containing reading material linked to each. Many offer imposing views of nearby landmarks, such as St Anne's Church; all have safes, internet connections and underfloor bathroom heating, while the more expensive have AC. The Sonnets restaurant is one of the classiest and most expensive in Vilnius. The bar is of course called The Globe, where the drinks are pricey but the sofas so soft you'll have to concentrate while in company to prevent yourself nodding off. Try one of the Gothic-style desserts on the opulent menu. *Sgls 360–720Lt, dbls 600–760Lt.*

MID-RANGE HOTELS

These hotels are of two- or three-star standard.

Ambassador Gedimino 12; ↘ (5) 261 5450; f (5) 212 1716; e info@ambassador.lt; www.ambassador.lt [1 D2]

Handily located on the city's main street, this hotel has recently (2004) completed a modernisation that slowly started years before. Unusually for a hotel in this category, several rooms have baths, rather than just showers. Its location combined with its price make it very sought after in the summer, when it is often fully booked months in advance. The café/restaurant on the ground floor keeps busy throughout the day and evening. Like the hotel, it is straightforward and functional, without any pretensions. *Sgls 240Lt, dbls 280Lt, trpls 340Lt, suites 360Lt.*

Apia Šv Ignoto 12; ☎ (5) 212 3426; f (5) 212 3618; e apia@apia.lt; www.apia.lt [I E4]
Wafer-thin and reasonably priced, the Apia allows you to squeeze into the very centre of the Old Town at no great expense to your wallet. If you're not bothered about a minibar, but need the option of satellite TV, this is for you. *Dbls 28Lt, suites 330Lt.*

Balatonas Latvių 38; ☎ (5) 272 2250; f (5) 272 2134; e info@balatonas.lt; www.balatonas.lt [*Vilnius* map]
A small, easy-going favourite with visiting middle-class eastern European businessmen, the Hungarian-owned Balatonas is a pearly white villa located in the leafy Žvėrynas district, close to several embassies. *Sgls 160–205Lt, dbls 195–260Lt, suites 260–340Lt, apartments 340–405Lt.*

Baltpark Ukmergės 363; ☎ (5) 238 800; f (5) 238 8555; e vilnius@baltpark.com; www.baltpark.com
You can't miss this 83-room hotel, a bright-blue building on the road to Riga that stands out against the surrounding Soviet-era high-rises. If you don't mind staying right at the far edge of the city, the Baltpark boasts unpretentious, friendly service and spotlessly clean rooms.

Most bizarre is the special 'Trio Lux' lighting in every room, which 'creates your own mood'. Choose from a combination of reds, greens and blues to make shades of calming colours. *Dbls 229Lt, suites 349Lt.*

Business Guest House Saltoniškių 44; ↳ (5) 272 2298; f (5) 275 3761; e info@bgh.lt; www.bgh.lt [*Vilnius* map]
Set on the bustling northern edge of Žvėrynas close to a main road, the atmosphere inside is Scandinavian and efficient, with business services, sauna, swimming pool, even a commercial art gallery. *Sgls 224Lt, dbls 260Lt, suites 345Lt.*

Comfort Gėlių 5; ↳ (5) 264 8833; f (5) 264 8832; e reservation@takas.lt; www.comfort.lt [3 E7]
With 57 rooms and a location about a 10-min walk from the Old Town, this hotel will suit groups and individuals wanting low prices but reasonable standards and location. The immediate vicinity is dull, but life and colour are not far away. *Sgls 110Lt, dbls 130Lt.*

Domus Maria Aušros Vartų 12; ↳ (5) 264 4880; f (5) 264 4878; e domusmaria@vilnensis.lt; www.domusmaria.vilnensis.lt [4 G6]
This is officially a guesthouse but feels like a hotel. Most of its 39 rooms were formerly monastery cells but those days are long past, although its position on a courtyard immediately behind the St Theresa Church gives it a serenity which will appeal to those wanting a quiet central location. The lounge on the 5th floor has extensive views over the Old Town. The restaurant offers perhaps the closest link to the past with the only decoration on the walls being a crucifix, but it looks down on a well-stocked bar. *Sgls 160Lt, dbls 220Lt.*

Ecotel Slucko 8; ℩ (5) 210 2700; f (5) 210 2707; e hotel@ecotel.lt; www.ecotel.lt [*Vilnius* map]

Another example of a hotel aiming at a combination of modernity and economy. It occupies a former shoe factory between the new business district and the Žalgiris Stadium so a 10-min walk is needed to reach anything of interest. Among its unusual features are special rooms for allergy sufferers and extra-long beds for tall people. Expect to see lots of sports groups here. *Sgls 170Lt, dbls 190Lt, trpls 210Lt.*

Europa City Jasinskio 14; ℩ (5) 251 4477; f (5) 251 4476; e city@hoteleuropa.lt; www.hoteleuropa.lt [*Vilnius* map]

Although a sister hotel to Europa Royale, this newcomer is much larger and less exclusive and is bound to suffer in comparison. Nothing is wrong with it, but nothing entices either, and whatever the interior, the surroundings are so drab that it really can only suit business travellers rather than tourists. *Sgls 238Lt, dbls 273Lt, suites 342–376Lt, apartments 480Lt.*

Mikotel Pylimo 63; ℩ (5) 260 9626; f (5) 260 9627; e mikotel@takas.lt; www.mikotel.lt [4 F7]

When gentrification finally comes to Pylimo Street and its market, this hotel will be a lovely place to stay. For the time being, it is still an outpost of cleanliness and taste in surroundings that are the complete opposite. The self-catering facilities are a great asset for those wishing to cook some of their own meals and its location halfway between the Old Town and the stations means that some tourists never use a bus or taxi during their entire stay here. *Sgls 110Lt, dbls 140Lt, apartments 230–270Lt.*

Mid-range hotels

Panorama Sodų 14; ℡ (5) 273 8011; f (5) 216 3789; e reservation@hotelpanorama.lt; www.hotelpanorama.lt [3 E8]

For years this was the notorious Gintaras, which seemed oblivious to all the surrounding changes, so sensible travellers who had just come into the bus station rushed by on the way to something more salubrious in town. Now all has changed and one has to wonder why it could not have done so ten years ago. Anyway, its 200 rooms can now be recommended, particularly those on the top floor which have the best views over the Old Town. Photographers should ask to get onto the roof to record them. Others can simply stay in the bar to enjoy the scenery. There is a bank in the foyer so no need to go out to look for better exchange rates. *Sgls 90–139Lt, dbls 120–169Lt, trpls 139–249Lt, suites 159–249Lt.*

Senatoriai Tilto 2; ℡ (5) 212 6491 or 212 7056; f (5) 212 6372; e senator@takas.lt; www.senatoriai.com [1 E2]

This small low-rise hotel profits from an excellent location, being discreetly tucked away down a side street immediately to the rear of Gedimino, just a stone's throw from the cathedral. *Sgls 150–250Lt, dbls 300–350Lt.*

BUDGET HOTELS AND GUESTHOUSES

These establishments have either one or two stars, or else have no official categorisation.

Bernadinų (11 rooms) Bernardinų 5; ℡ (5) 261 5134; f (5) 260 84 21; e guesthouse@avevita.lt/guesthouse; www.avevita.lt/guesthouse [2 C4]

Offering peace and quiet in the Old Town at a very reasonable price, this is a new guesthouse close to St Anne's Church. Pay a little extra for breakfast and parking in the courtyard. Some rooms are bigger and come with small kitchens. *Sgls 120Lt, dbls 150Lt, trpls 215Lt, suites 230Lt, apartments 400Lt; these prices are reduced by 50% out of season. Breakfast is 7Lt extra.*

Jeruzalė (10 rooms) Kalvarijų 209; \ (5) 271 4040; f (5) 276 2627; e jeruzale@takas.lt; www.jeruzale.com
Comfortable budget option 10 mins' drive from the centre, not far from the Calvary Church and trails in the forest. The low price of these 10 rooms means you can splash out on taxis every day – or catch buses 26, 35, 36 or 50. *Sgls 100Lt, dbls 100–142Lt, suites 214–256Lt.*

Pušis Blindzių 17; \ (5) 268 3939; f (5) 272 1305; e pusis@pusishotel.lt; www.pusishotel.lt
[*Vilnius* map]
A basic, one-star hotel in Žvėrynas popular in season with Polish tour groups, but quiet out of season and close to lovely Vingis Park. *Sgls 70Lt, dbls 100Lt, suites 170Lt.*

Victoria Saltoniškių 56; \ (5) 272 4013; f (5) 272 4320; e hotel@victoria.lt; www.victoria.lt
[*Vilnius* map]
When this first opened in the mid-1990s it was a welcome and necessary addition to the Vilnius hotel scene with bright décor and friendly service. It now has price and car-parking space going for it, but not much else given that what was novel 10 years ago is now standard throughout Vilnius. *Sgls 124–190Lt, dbls 159–207Lt, suites 204–238Lt.*

HOSTELS

AAA Hostel (24 beds) Šv. Stepono 15; ☎ 680 18557; e info@ahostel.lt [3 D7]
A new hostel run by a well-known local real estate and accommodation company, the AAA has Internet access, Old Town location, safe lockers – the hostelling works. *Dorm bed 31Lt.*

IYHF Filaretai Hostel Filaretų 17; ☎ (5) 215 4627; f (5) 212 0149;
e info@filaretaihostel.lt [*Vilnius* map]
It's a 20-minute hike from the bus station out to this hostel in the bohemian district of Užupis, but the friendly, lively atmosphere is worth the sweat. You might even be lucky enough to get one of the 5 cheap doubles. *Dorm bed 28–32Lt, sgls 65Lt, dbls 90Lt, with a 5Lt reduction per person from second night.*

IYHF Old Town Hostel Aušros Vartų 20-10; ☎ (5) 262 5357; f (5) 268 5967;
e oldtownhostel@delfi.lt; www.balticbackpackers.com
The much smaller of Vilnius's two IYHF-affiliated hostels is actually just outside the confines of the Old Town, close to the railway station. *Dorm bed 32Lt.*

Jaunujų Turistų Centras (50 beds) Polocko 7; ☎ (5) 261 3576; f (5) 262 7742 [*Vilnius* map]
Basic hostel in the Užupis district overlooking the bubbling River Vilnia. Rooms are for three or four people. Parking on the premises, but unlike the other hostels little English is spoken. *Dorm bed 26Lt.*

BED AND BREAKFAST

Litinterp Bernardinų 7/2; ☏ (5) 212 3850; f (5) 212 3559; e vilnius@litinterp.com;
www.litinterp.com [2 G3]
Open Mon–Fri 08.30–17.30, Sat 09.00–15.30. This hostel became famous when it opened and
has kept ahead of most attempts to compete with it. The location, price and self-catering
facilities make it ideal for those wanting a basic but impeccably clean base in the Old Town,
although some rooms are very possibly the tiniest in town. The company also offers rooms
in private houses in central Vilnius and Trakai, and has some apartments for rent. Advance
bookings for Kaunas, Klaipėda, Palanga and Nida can be made, and car hire, interpretation
and translation services are available. *Sgls 80–100Lt, dbls 120–160Lt, trpls 180–210Lt.*

Bed and breakfast

Eating and drinking

The pleasure of dining in Vilnius today is that there is such an unexpected wealth of different kinds of restaurants, all of them striving to be original. It's partly because of the amazing culinary revolution that has taken place since the dull Soviet years that it is so easy to be impressed when you go out for a meal. The art of providing a romantic or a lively evening meal, even the ideal business lunch, is being perfected right across the capital. European and broadly international cuisine dominates, so as not to upset local palates too much, and traditional Lithuanian dishes like the uniquely weighty *cepelinai* are available in an increasing number of rustic-style theme restaurants that are as popular with the locals as they are with visitors. There are some strange absences, however. Asian cuisine is almost exclusively taken up by an inexplicable number of Chinese restaurants, some of them better than others. There is nothing Malaysian or Thai apart from the odd dish on an international menu or rare bursts of 'fusion'. One brave retired Indian air force commander, Rajinder Chaudhary, has struggled with his excellent Indian restaurant, Sue's Indian Raja, in four different locations in the last ten years, and still attracts only expats and tourists. But Vilnius is not just meat and potatoes. Greater awareness about healthy eating ensures that tasty, attractively presented salads are especially easy to find. With one or two exceptions, such as the pricey La Provence, there is not a great deal of variation in what you can expect to pay at the restaurants listed. The price of a three-course meal for two, excluding wine, should come to around 120–180Lt. For bars and clubs, see page 95.

RESTAURANTS

Belmonto Kriokliai Belmonto 17; www.belmontas.lt

Incredible amalgamation of both indoor and open-air folk-style theme eateries, the excellent Vila Gloria restaurant, refreshing waterfall, beautiful countryside and space for everything from conferences to weddings – all just a 15-min taxi ride from the centre of Vilnius.

Čagino Basanavičiaus 11; ✆ (5) 261 5555

For authentic Russian dishes and, on Fri and Sat, 'Russian romance' played by a solitary musician with a guitar and a portfolio of popular, sing-along songs, venture a few mins' walk away from the Old Town to this atmospheric subterranean hideaway.

Čili Didžioji 5 and Gedimino 23; www.cili.lt [2 F4]

Wander into one of these branches of the phenomenally successful local Čili chain and you'll quickly discover how pizza has become the Lithuanian fast food of choice. But not why. The service is quick and the salads adequate, but the pizzas are nothing really special.

Čili Kaimas Vokiečių 8 and Gedimino 14; ✆ (5) 231 2536 [3 E5] [1 D2]

Two among a plethora of new theme restaurants offering traditional Lithuanian food, these boast live chickens, pitchforks and even a country-style granny employed full-time at the Gedimino outlet to knit in front of diners. Some people will love Čili Kaimas, run by the popular Lithuanian pizza chain, for its culinary authenticity and its prices. Others will call it village kitsch.

Da Antonio Vilniaus 23 and Pilies 20; www.antonio.lt [1 C2] [2 G3]
Excellent Italian dishes served at tables in a pleasantly decorated yet secluded seating arrangement. Come to this quite authentic *trattoria* rather than the homegrown Čili outlets if you fancy a real pizza and bottle of good Italian wine.

El Gaucho Sano Pilies 10; ↘ (5) 210 7773 [2 G3]
With an unbeatable combination of relaxing atmosphere, spacious seating, meaty food and reliable service, this restaurant set inside the atrium of the Atrium Hotel claims to be Argentinian. That's debatable. But it's certainly perfect for an evening meal with good wine.

Ephesus Trakų 15; ↘ (5) 260 8866 [1 D4]
Although open until 06.00 every night except Sun, when it closes early at 01.00, this is in fact a conventional Turkish restaurant which has imported not only its menu but also its prices and its generous portions. Even water pipes are available to stress its difference from contemporary Lithuania.

Fortas Gedimino 37; ↘ (5) 249 6030
If you happen to be around the central part of Gedimino Avenue and you need an easy bite that's not too challenging, the chain-pub-style Fortas offers an eclectic range of dishes.

Forto Dvaras Pilies 16; ↘ (5) 261 1070 [2 G3]
A warren of rooms under bustling Pilies Street that offer traditional Lithuanian cuisine such

as the famously stodgy *cepelinai* and also *vederai* – pig intestines stuffed with mashed potato. You might even learn what the difference is between Samogitian and Lithuanian food.

Freskos Didžioji 31; ☎ (5) 261 8133 [4 F5]

One of the great survivors of the Vilnius dining scene, Freskos has seen better days. Housed at the rear end of the Town Hall, it is still popular with expats and diplomats who have litas to spare, and still has a regularly changing menu with dishes to please. But the theatrical décor has worn a little at the edges.

Ibish Aušros Vartų 11; ☎ (8) 651 98879 [4 G6]

The name is Turkish, but there's little that is genuinely Turkish about this new restaurant close to the Gates of Dawn. Instead, this 'lounge restaurant' boasts more than 100 cocktails to accompany your meal. Try the grilled salmon, which is accentuated by smoky bacon on a bed of lentils and carrots, adorned with lime.

IdaBasar Subačiaus 3; www.idabazar.lt [4 G6]

Another of Vilnius's long-time survivors, IdaBasar relies on hearty German cuisine mainstays – and good German beer – to compete with the fresher newcomers. Not a bad option at the southern edge of the Old Town.

Kineret Raugyklos 4; ☎ (5) 233 5648 [3 D7]

Despite the fact that 40% of the population of Vilnius was Jewish before 1941, Kineret gave the city its first real taste of kosher food when it opened in 2005. There are no meat dishes, just high-quality fish and vegetable courses served with wine from Israel and cosy

Restaurants

surroundings. In the inner atrium of the building that houses Kineret, you can still see what remains of Hebrew lettering on what was once the shopfront of a bakery.

Kinija Konstitucijos 12; ☎ (5) 263 6363
Possibly the best of Vilnius's countless Chinese restaurants, Kinija is located across the river from the Old Town, close to the landmark Reval Hotel Lietuva. The broccoli, aubergine and seafood dishes really stand out. Wash them down with a large bottle of gassy Tsingtao beer.

Kristupo Kavinė Pilies 24; ☎ (5) 261 7722 [2 G3]
Though it is called 'Christopher's Café', this is really a classy restaurant next door to the Narutis Hotel on the Old Town's main drag. Rarely crowded, however, it offers beautifully presented dishes on rustic-style linen tablecloths, overlooked by framed sketches of sophisticated couples from the Roaring Twenties.

La Provence Vokiečių 24; www.laprovence.lt [3 E5]
Advertising itself as '100% pure gourmet', this relatively pricey restaurant sandwiched between the two constituent parts of the far more informal Žemaičiai serves Provençal and other Mediterranean cuisines. The number of French-speakers regularly to be found here is proof of the high standards and extensive wine list.

Les Amis Savičiaus 9; ☎ (5) 212 3738 [4 G5]
The best of provincial France has finally reached Vilnius. The family do the cooking and waiting and the menu reflects what could be bought fresh during the day. It's a popular spot, so reserve ahead.

Literatų Svetainė Gedimino 1; www.literatai.lt [1 E2]

With a view from your candlelit table to the cathedral and a meal prepared by some of the best chefs in Vilnius, the 'Literary Salon' specialises in modern (ie: healthy and not stodgy) Scandinavian cuisine with a good choice of wines. This has been a café for many years. It was from one of these windows that Czeslaw Milosz, the Nobel-Prize-winning poet, witnessed Soviet tanks occupy the city in June 1940.

Lokys Stiklių 8; www.lokys.lt [4 F5]

One of the few survivors from Soviet times, 'The Bear' has updated its service standards but not its menu. It is a must for the enthusiastic carnivore. Boar, elk, even bear itself are on the menu. Eat in one of the tiny rooms carved out of the cellar, or on the ground floor in the shadow of a stuffed grizzly. The reasonably priced lunch menu is good quality, although a 20-minute wait is necessary.

Mano Guru Vilniaus 22; ☏ (5) 212 0126 [1 D3]

This restaurant achieved instant success when it was revealed that all the staff were reformed drug addicts and that Mayor Zuokas had promoted this project having seen the success of the idea in Prague. The variety of food is such that one is willing to sacrifice alcohol and to leave by 20.30 which is the state of play here. Fresh fruit and vegetables which seem unavailable elsewhere all turn up with every dish and although meat and fish are served, they almost seem redundant. Puréed soup and the vegetarian main courses are more than enough. Smoking is understandably banned here, a pleasant rarity in Vilnius even in 2006.

Marceliukės Klėtis Tuskulėnų 35; ☎ (5) 272 5087

Probably the most tongue-in-cheek of the traditional Lithuanian restaurants, and the longest running, this is off the beaten track in a bizarre setting of high-rises a short taxi ride from the centre. The hearty portions, merry atmosphere, live folk music and smiling service are worth the journey.

Markus ir Ko Antokolskio 11; ☎ (5) 262 3185 [2 F4]

A relaxing, jazzy atmosphere, live piano music and succulent steaks on one of the Old Town's tiniest streets.

Medininkai Aušros Vartų 8; ☎ (5) 266 0771 [4 G6]

The chefs here like to call the cuisine 'Lithuanian fusion', using imaginative ways to prepare and present traditional local food. With vaulted ceilings littered with frescoes, 18th-century Italian artwork and a peaceful red-brick courtyard open in summer, the Medininkai makes the most of its location in a former monastery near the Gates of Dawn. Another plus is that it is now under the reliable management of the adjoining Hotel Europa Royale.

Rojaus Arka Daukšos 3; ☎ (5) 212 0625 [4 G7]

Often forgotten since it lies just beyond the tourist trail the other side of the Gates of Dawn, the 'Arch of Paradise' is easy to spot because of its ornately carved doorway. Inside, settle into the quiet, comfortable atmosphere and choose from a short menu of Lithuanian-style dishes.

Rossini L Stuokos-Gucevičiaus 1; ☎ (5) 210 7466 [1 E2]

Adjoining the Hotel CityPark opposite the cathedral, but with its own separate entrance, Rossini benefits enormously from having one of Vilnius's best-known chefs, Enzo Recupero, who regularly appears in the dining area to add an entertaining panache to the excellent Italian dishes being served.

Rytai Naugarduko 22 and Gedimino 49a; ☎ (5) 249 6655

Two of Vilnius's better Chinese restaurants, one near the Parliament, the other on the New Town's eastern edge. Inexpensive delights include a thick, rich chilli seafood soup and a squid dish that comes with oyster sauce and hot paprika. Ask for extra spice.

Saint Germain Literatu 9; ☎ (5) 262 1210 [2 G3]

This charming little rustic French-style restaurant opened in spring 2005, promoting wine above all else, but also serving fabulous food. It has shelves haphazardly crammed with books and somehow managed immediately to appear old and settled. In the unlikely event that guests prefer to take away the wine rather than drink it on the premises, many varieties are sold by the bottle.

San Marco Subačiaus 2; ☎ (5) 264 6418 [4 G6]

The new, elegant, centrally situated San Marco restaurant brings creative Italian cuisine to Vilnius in a Mediterranean setting. Opposite the National Philharmonic, it's an excellent choice for a first-class business lunch or evening dining.

Solero Trakų 7; ☎ (5) 260 8696 [1 D4]

Suddenly, two restaurants appeared in 2005 introducing Spanish cuisine to Vilnius. This is the better, more central of the two, offering delightful tapas like Tabla de Embutidos y Quesos, a delicious plate of Spanish cheeses and Serrano ham, as well as paella, salads and sangria.

Sorena Islandijos 4; ☏ (5) 262 7560 [1 C3]
Vilnius's only restaurant featuring genuinely authentic cuisine from Azerbaijan, Sorena has slowly earned a reputation for its mouthwatering Caucasian food and friendly service. Named after a heroic army leader in the early history of Persia, there is also an Iranian element to the decoration and the food. Try the Tebriz, a tender roll of beef served on a skewer with a crisp green chilli pepper.

Sorrento Pylimo 21; ☏ (5) 264 4737 [3 C5]
A calm haven of expensive Italian dining that is in strange contrast to the rest of busy, low-key Pylimo Street. The wood-fired oven by the bar is responsible for some delicious pizzas.

Stiklių Aludė, Gaono 7; ☏ (5) 262 4501 [2 F4]
Run by the plush Stikliai Hotel, the price difference between this beautifully decorated cellar-level tavern and the ultra-posh French restaurant next door seems to be getting wider all the time. The Aludė combines reasonably priced Lithuanian food with good service.

Sue's Indian Raja Odminių 3; ☏ (8) 600 27788 [1 E2]
Ideally situated opposite Vilnius Cathedral, Sue's offers authentic Indian cuisine that is ahead of its time in the Baltics. If you want hot spices, the Madras and Jhalfarezi dishes will not disappoint, but even for seasoned tastes there will be something special. Try the Fish Amritsari, dipped in a masala of spices and herbs and deep fried.

Tores Užupio 40; www.tores.lt [2 J4]

The website, although only in Lithuanian, is so visually dramatic that it is worth watching in its own right. This restaurant manages to reinvent itself several times a day. At lunch during the week, it is probably best to be over 40 and to have plenty of time. These visitors come for the view. Early in the evening the clientele are there to be seen, so can drop in age to around 30. Later an even younger set take over and probably have to be asked to leave at 02.00 which is closing time. Generations do however mix over lunch at weekends, particularly in the summer, when children can play outside.

Vandens Malūnas Verkių 100; ╲ (5) 271 1666

Occupying a converted 19th-century watermill in Verkiai Park, this is a popular excursion destination, particularly in summer, when three outdoor terraces are open. Traditional Lithuanian fare is served, and there is a good line in freshwater fish dishes.

Žaldokynė Molėtai Rd; ╲ (8) 655 09601

One of growing number of out-of-town country inns serving traditional food served in a fun, barn-house atmosphere. This one is 17km north of Vilnius on the road to Molėtai, easily reached by taxi. Go for the Žaldoko Appetiser, a clay dish of sausage, bacon, gherkins, salad and a shot of the house's very own homemade vodka.

Žemaičiai Vokiečių 24; ╲ (5) 261 6573 [3 E5]

Descend a hazardous flight of steps into a world of traditional food and furnishings from western Lithuania. The choice of seating ranges from throne-like chairs to country-home beds. Expect starchy food and good beer.

Restaurants

CAFÉS

Balti Drambliai Vilniaus 41; ☎ (5) 242 0875 [1 D4]

Hard to define, 'White Elephants' is a cellar-level vegetarian café-restaurant with a no-smoking policy but plenty to imbibe. There's also an Indian touch to the décor, which includes a magnificent bar with an elephant's head fashioned out of it.

Bar Italia Gedimino 3a; ☎ (5) 268 5824 [1 E2]

Squeeze into this tiny but polished caffeine pit-stop close to the cathedral for your espresso, a snack and fresh fruit juice.

Café de Paris Didžioji 1; ☎ (5) 261 1021 [2 F4]

Café-restaurant attached to the French Cultural Centre; it has a predictably good choice of crêpes and great coffee, but a totally un-French selection of loud background music which may drown out conversation. It's also getting a little worn at the seams.

Casa del Caffè Gedimino 1; ☎ (5) 261 1461 [1 E2]

Bright, cheerful café tucked just around the corner from Gedimino, on Tilto Street. The buns and coffee are delicious. But it attracts the odd hobo.

Collegium Pilies 22; ☎ (5) 261 8334 [2 G3]

There is no more convenient place for public Internet access in central Vilnius than this cybercafé, which charges 8Lt per hour and is open 08.00–midnight.

Double Coffee Pilies 34, Gedimino 5 and 26; ☎ (5) 261 4175 [2 G4] [1 E2]

By the time this book is published there will doubtless be several other addresses in Vilnius as this chain expands rapidly throughout the Baltics. Prices are very non-Baltic, in fact rather too British, but clients probably accept this in return for the consistently high quality of the drinks and the service.

Gabi Šv Mykolo 6; ☎ (5) 212 3643 [2 G3]
A homely retreat on one the Old Town's quietest streets offering unadventurous Lithuanian meals in a fireside atmosphere. Next door is the Amber Museum and St Anne's Church is a few steps away.

Pauzė Aušros Vartų 5; ☎ (5) 212 2113 [4 G6]
Point to whatever fresh cakes or buns you fancy and take them with coffee or tea. Savory dishes are quickly microwaved. 'Pause' overlooks the busy square in front of the Filharmonija, so the window seats – and especially the balcony in summer – are pleasant for people-watching.

Pieno Baras Didžioji 21; ☎ (5) 269 0991 [4 F5]
It is amazing how this old café dating from the Soviet days keeps on running. Probably because of its cheap prices and popularity with students. Line up for buns, coffee or cocoa and try to find a seat. Don't expect to find wireless Internet here.

Ponių Laimė Stiklių 14; ☎ (5) 264 9581 [1 E4]
One of the best Old Town cafés for delicious cakes and biscuits with original recipes, 'Ladies' Happiness' is popular with men too. It's also good for lunch, with basic meals on display, weighed and microwaved.

Cafés

Presto Pilies 24; ☎ (5) 210 7779 [2 G2]

With its prominent position on Pilies Street, this is one of the more obvious, less atmospheric choices for freshly ground imported coffees and teas – and cakes, breakfast and beer too.

Prie Angelo Užupio 9; ☎ (5) 215 3790 [2 J4]

Once part of the arty Užupis district's enigmatic ruins, this is now a richly decorated café serving inexpensive lunches. Found next to the angel statue, it makes for a convenient break while exploring Užupis's oddities.

Radom Domininkonų 16; ☎ (5) 212 0918 [2 F4]

Tiny café near the university. Often convenient for a quick bite, but the buns are sometimes not so fresh.

Skonis ir Kvapas Trakų 8; ☎ (5) 212 2803 [1 D4]

It feels like an upmarket tearoom, tastefully decorated, with teas and coffees from around the world on display. Hidden in a courtyard, it's hugely popular, friendly and serves great meals too.

Sole Luna Universiteto 4; ☎ (5) 212 0925 [2 F3]

Situated alongside the university, this Italian café is a particularly recommendable choice for a summertime alfresco drink with a salami and mozzarella ciabatta, which can be enjoyed in the irregularly shaped triple-tier Baroque courtyard to the rear. Beer is cheaper before 21.00 every evening, but this is the place to enjoy four varieties of grappa or the 30 different wines which sell for less than £10/US$19 a bottle.

Soprano Pilies 2; ☏ (5) 212 6042 [2 G3]
For delightful ice cream on a hot day, Soprano is the best parlour in town. But if it's chilly, just take their excellent coffee.

Užupio Užupio 2; ☏ (5) 212 2138 [2 H4]
Predictably, the 'local' of Vilnius's bohemian quarter is a favourite with artists and students. Idyllically set by the River Vilnia, it has a spacious beer garden (the only one in Vilnius) and a contrastingly cosy interior, which makes the walk there in winter quite acceptable. Do not be surprised to see the Mayor of Vilnius, Artūras Zuokas, drop in from time to time, even though he could surely afford more lavish surroundings nowadays. Perhaps he likes the deliberately old-fashioned décor, which is such a contrast to the working environment he has established for the council and for the business community on the other side of the Neris River.

Užupio Klasika Užupio 28; ☏ (5) 215 3677 [2 J4]
With its top-quality Segafredo coffee and an assortment of homemade pancakes, salads and pasta dishes, this tiny, five-table café is the perfect pause for breath on a daytime amble through the city. When more than eight people are waiting for food, you may be there for a while. But the relaxed atmosphere and music are somehow conducive to conversation, or to reading the newspaper – or perusing your guidebook for that matter.

Viena Trakų 5; ☏ (5) 261 1257 [3 D5]
Native American cake expert Franklin Orosco opened this wonderful, casual-minded café in 2005. All the coffee is freshly ground and not kept beyond 14 days after removing from the

Cafés

vacuum packaging. The almond cookies are divine, the Linzer Torte delectable. Great milk shakes, sandwiches and chilli con carne too.

Žaltvykslė Pilies 11; ☎ (5) 268 7173 [2 G3]

This establishment, named after a grass-snake, sells itself as a Hungarian restaurant, but is really just an old-fashioned café with cheap meals, popular with university students. These days, there are better places to eat or drink on Pilies Street.

Church of St Michael

Ententainment and nightlife

Vilnius at night is unrecognisable from the quiet backwater is was ten years ago. Dozens of sweaty, pumping new nightspots and atmospheric watering holes seem to open every year, pushing the boundaries of the city centre westwards along Gedimino and eastwards into Užupis. For pre- or post-club relaxation, there is a greater choice of chillout zones, often off the beaten track. At weekends, opening hours extend beyond daylight. Clubbing is in; folk dancing is most definitely out.

There is still plenty of demand for chamber orchestras, contemporary dance, theatre, opera and ballet, however, and there is no more evocative city to combine a concert and an excellent evening meal than Vilnius.

Hardly a week passes in Vilnius without a cultural festival of one sort or another taking place. Unlike in many other capitals of Eastern Europe, these continue through the summer and on into autumn. Whilst the occasional artist from abroad may be engaged to participate, such is the diversity of talent available in Lithuania itself, that even someone from Kaunas or Klaipėda might be seen as an outsider. *VilniusNOW!*, *Vilnius in Your Pocket* and the *Baltic Times* are the best local sources in print for information on events.

OPERA, BALLET AND CONCERTS
Inside the colossal **Lithuanian Opera and Ballet Theatre** (*Vienuolio 1;* ✆ *(5) 262 0727; www.opera.lt*), three or four performances a week are held in a

programme that is fixed about six months ahead. This extraordinary example of overblown Brezhnev-era architecture hasn't changed structurally, its huge chandeliers still glaring through monumental windows, but fortunately its productions have, with frequent new productions mingling with old favourites. Vilnius attracts some world-class performers, often Russian, though not quite as many as Riga.

Ticket prices are very reasonable, ranging from 10Lt to 120Lt. Operas and ballets are highly popular, but such is the size of the venue it is usually possible to buy tickets once you arrive in Vilnius. The ticket office can be found inside a door at the bottom of the building facing the river. Performances are normally in the original language, with some being contemporary Lithuanian works. The opera is closed in July and August.

The Opera and Ballet Theatre benefits from regular charitable donations from various countries and international corporations, enough to guarantee replacement of some outdated equipment every year. Plush new seats embossed with the opera logo were installed in summer 2005.

The best classical music concerts are held at the **Congress Palace** (*Vilniaus 6;* ℩ *(5) 261 8828*), where the Lithuanian State Symphony Orchestra teams up with local and international musical personages for concerts held throughout the year, except in summer, and the **National Philharmonic Hall** (*Aušros Vartų 5;* ℩ *266 5216* [4 F6]), the city's most impressive concert hall, which hosts everything from pianists and quartets by renowned foreign musicians to full-blown orchestral extravaganzas. On a smaller scale, the **Music Academy** (*Gedimino 42;* ☎ *261 2691*) students and professors give free-of-charge recitals on weekdays during term time.

Always look out for the **St Christopher Chamber Orchestra**, founded in 1994, which brings together several young chamber ensembles, string quartets and solo performers. Its brilliant concerts are performed at different venues in Vilnius as well as abroad.

In addition, concerts and organ recitals are held in several Old Town churches, especially the cathedral, St John's and St Casimir's. At the latter, live music is normally performed every Sunday immediately after the last morning mass ends at around 13.00. Open-air concerts – which take place in the courtyards of Vilnius University and the Chodkevičius Palace, among other venues – are a regular feature of the city's musical life in summertime.

The main venue for large-scale pop concerts is now the **Siemens Arena** (*Ozo 14; www.siemens-arena.com*), a new multipurpose event and conference centre that opened in 2004 opposite the Akropolis shopping complex. In the Old Town, **Tamsta** (*Subačiaus 11a;* ☎ *212 4498* [4 G6]) has built up a reputation for great live blues, rock, hip hop and even gospel, its hip, bohemian and very friendly atmosphere open to any influences. **Brodvėjus** (*Mėsinių 4;* ☎ *210 7208*) is more of a beery pub venue, its younger fanbase bopping around to regular live concerts of local rock music, jazz and blues. The best venue for international and local DJs is **Gravity** (*Jasinskio 16; www.clubgravity.lt*), open only at weekends and famed for its location in a Soviet-era bomb shelter.

Opera, ballet and concerts

FILMS AND THEATRE

State-of-the-art multiplexes now dominate the city's film-going scene. The last of the fondly remembered old Soviet-era cinemas are being sold and repackaged. The Lietuva on Pylimo is being turned into shops, the Pergalė on Pamėkalnio has to become a new casino and restaurant and the Helios on Didžioji is now an entertainment complex of restaurants, nightclub and strip joint. The last non-multiplex survivor, the Skalvijos opposite the Green Bridge, goes under the hammer in 2006.

There are two multiplexes to choose from in Vilnius, both offering films in the original language with Lithuanian subtitles. An evening out at the cinema is therefore a good evening entertainment option for tourists, though the diet of big-budget Hollywood movies will not appeal to everyone. Check www.forumcinemas.lt or ☎ 1567 to find out what's on, where and when. **Coca-Cola Plaza**, also known by its old name the Vingis Cinema, has 12 screens and almost 2,000 seats (including a few dozen for the disabled) a short taxi ride from the Old Town at Savanorių 8. A little further away, Forum Cinemas has a second multiplex at the gigantic Akropolis shopping centre.

The **Cinema Spring** festival is an increasingly interesting, week-long annual movie festival with films from around the world, usually taking place in March.

The language barrier should not be seen as a hindrance in the theatre. Many productions are, of course, of foreign classics which will be known to visitors and in other cases the ticket prices are so low that it is worth staying for at least the first act simply to see Lithuanian drama literally in action. The **National Drama Theatre** (*Gedimino 4;* ☏ 262 977) is the city's biggest theatrical stage, used for plays, modern dance, avant-garde productions and festivals. A statue of three ghostly muses graces the entrance. New management at the **Russian Drama Theatre** (*Basanavičiaus 13;* ☏ 262 7133) has brought in a more varied programme than just Russian-language performances, while the **Small State Theatre of Vilnius** (*Gedimino 22;* ☏ (5) 261 3125; *www.vmt.lt/en*) is a new stage with repertoire ranging from Chekhov to contemporary Lithuanian plays. The **Youth Theatre** (*Arklių 5;* ☏ 261 6126) shows cutting-edge plays and innovative productions staged by some of Lithuania's best writers and directors.

Finally, the **Lėlė Puppet Theatre** (*Arklių 5;* ☏ 262 8678 [4 G6]) is a unique and entertaining festival of puppetry for children of all ages – and adults too. Located inside the Baroque Oginskis Palace, like the Youth Theatre, it has managed to stay open through good times and bad since it was founded in the 1950s.

BARS AND CLUBS

A revolution has taken place in the last five years. Vilnius now offers a wide range of options for the evening and early morning hours. It's no longer just boom-boom techno. DJs play as much cool jazz and lounge music as they do throbbing performances of light and noise. Bars, meanwhile, range from old-fashioned, fireside pubs like Aukštaičiai and Prie Universiteto to more colourfully designed watering holes like Savas Kampas. Cozy, Paparazzi and Pabo Latino are more modern, club-style venues with tasteful, unintrusive chillout sounds, where you can mingle a little conversation with a little dancing and, in the case of the first two, extremely good food.

Amatininkų Užeiga Didžioji 19

A prominent location ensures that this tavern gets a tidy turnover, but the emphasis is on bar food and the beverage of choice is beer. If that's what you want, and you're quick enough to grab one of the tightly squeezed tables on the pavement out front in summer, then this may not quite fall under the label 'tourist trap'.

Artistai Šv Kazimiero 3; www.artistai.lt

The large, buzzing courtyard is the reason to come to this bar and relax during summer sunsets. But a comfortable interior, friendly service and Elvis recurring in the rock 'n' roll music selection should be enough to push you to venture down atmospheric Šv Kazimiero Street in winter too.

Aukštaičiai Antokolskio 13; www.aukstaiciai.lt

Popular with expats and the occasional stag group, this cavern of rooms is also a haven of tasty homemade food, ale made on the premises, entertaining open-mic nights and live music – usually one man squeezed into a tight corner surrounded by tables full of jolly folk, young and old.

Avilys Gedimino 5; www.avilys.lt

A popular microbrewery in a cellar close to the cathedral, what you come for at the 'Beehive' is the honey-flavoured or ginseng-spiced beer. It certainly takes precedence over the food, which is tasty but hardly inspiring. The varied bar snacks, which include everything from garlic bread to prawns, may be a better bet to go with the drinks, while the hedonistic 1920s alcohol ads decorating the walls only encourage you to drink more.

Bix Etmonų 6; www.bix.lt
More for those with alternative tastes, this Tarantino-style bar with rock music was founded over ten years ago by the early-'90s Lithuanian group of the same name. Still an exciting venue for a beer, and perhaps even a lurch to the noisy drones on the cellar dancefloor.

Brodvėjus Mėsinių 4; www.brodvejus.lt
Attracting a youthful crowd of mostly raucous students, this informal, barn-style venue with regular shows of live music is a good option if you fancy a wild, spontaneous evening.

Cozy Domininkonų 10; www.cozy.lt
As comfortable and relaxing by evening and into the early hours as it is during the day for its morning coffee and well-proportioned meals, Cozy is a warm, glowing chillout zone.

Entertainment Bank Pamėnkalnio 7; www.pramogubankas.lt. Fun-seekers can dine, drink, dance or gamble the day and night away at this extravagant venue in two restaurants, two clubs, seven bars, and a casino without leaving the building.

Fashionclub Trakų 2; www.ftv.lt [1 C4]
This exclusive chain of European entertainment venues arrived in Vilnius in 2005 to offer romantic, health-conscious dining, a stylish cocktail bar and a club that hosts fashion shows

Bars and clubs

downstairs. Suitably, this building used to be an 18th-century mansion where glamorous balls highlighted the latest European fashions. The only problem today is the grating Fashion TV music and images beamed from flat-panel screens virtually everywhere you look.

Galaxy Konstitucijos 26; www.forumpalace.lt

The largest nightclub in Vilnius, which can absorb 1,000 people or more, opens only on Fri and Sat when it can be sure of this turnout. A privilege card offers discounts once 5,000Lt (£1,000 or US$1,900) has been spent which perhaps indicates the clientele it attracts. The opening until 05.00 makes this financial barrier quite easy to reach. Seating is pretty sparse, so book a table or keep dancing.

Grand Casino Vienuolio 4; www.grandcasino.lt

The sophisticated side of Vilnius's new 21st-century casino scene, the Canadian-run Grand Casino entertainment complex promised big things for connoisseurs of gambling and non-gamblers alike when it opened in 2004. Unfortunately, while the casino itself continues to house an attractive collection of card and dice games, the other constituent parts of the complex were temporarily closed at the time of writing due to a financial disagreement. Should the New Orleans nightclub, with its great lighting and entertaining DJs, and the excellent Tokyo restaurant reopen, we recommend both for a quality night out.

Gravity Jasinskio 16; www.clubgravity.lt

As famed for its location in a Soviet-era bomb shelter as it is for its international DJs, Gravity attracts young local celebs and a faithful crew of regular party-goers. Found down a

60m tunnel that raises the adrenalin with a thudding bass noise, Gravity is minimalistic and industrial in its décor and unrelenting in its clubbing energy.

Pabo Latino Trakų 3; www.pabolatino.lt
Highly popular with stylish 20-somethings, this Old Town nightclub is sumptuously decorated, often more along the lines of an Eastern harem than a Latino dance party, with billowing tents outside in summer and plush cushions and rugs inside. For interesting conversations with beautiful locals, head for the courtyard's wooden steps.

Paparazzi Totoriu 3; www.paparrazi.lt
Following a brilliantly publicised opening in early 2005, this bar certainly set itself up as the place for the pretentious under-30s to be seen. The bar area has conventional celebrity photos, though nobody seems to have thought about the irony of including Princess Diana in a bar of this name. Those, however, in the toilets will only 'appeal' to those with the most broad-minded of tastes.

Prie Universiteto (also known as The Pub or the Pub'as) Domininkonų 9; www.pub.lt
A busy expat hangout with English-style bar-food during the 1990s, the Pub then changed hands and the food and the music went rapidly downhill. Things are improving, however, and it's still the best venue to watch a live football game on the big screen. It even had a recent evening of alternative music dedicated to the late John Peel.

Prospekto Gedimino 2
Sometimes amazing, sometimes disappointing, Prospekto nevertheless has bags of

Bars and clubs

atmosphere, especially on the new 3rd-floor lounge, where free palm readings and massages occasionally take place on the comfy sofas.

Savas Kampas Vokiečių 4; www.savaskampas.lt
This popular bar serves a wide range of food, including tasty lunchtime hotpots on weekdays. Its cellar closed in early 2005, when the kitchen moved down there as Lithuanians are no longer so keen on eating in cellars. The décor in the expanded ground-floor dining area is as varied as the food.

SkyBar Konstitucijos 20 (inside the Reval Hotel Lietuva); www.revalhotels.com [*Vilnius* map]
Everybody's favourite cocktail-bar-with-a-view, SkyBar is located at the top of the towering, 22-floor Reval Hotel Lietuva. It opens only at 16.00, but it's where all tours of the city should start or end. Just make your way through the lobby to the speedy lifts on the right. As you enter the bar, seat yourself on the left-hand side for the best view of the neon-lit Vilnius panorama, gazed at through floor-to-ceiling windows.

GAY VILNIUS

In most countries in central and eastern Europe gay scenes have been slow to emerge since the legal restraints of the Soviet era were abolished. In culturally conservative Vilnius, there is barely a scene at all. The hostility the gay community faced in earlier times has still not been eradicated. Gay marches in nearby Warsaw and Riga in 2005 attracted at least twice as many people hurling homophobic abuse at those brave enough to turn up and demand gay rights. Vilnius has never even had a gay march.

The press is hardly leading the way. Occasionally, the daily newspaper *Respublika*, the local equivalent of *The Sun*, runs hysterical anti-gay and anti-Semitic articles written by its editors. The fact that the publication is barely prosecuted and that statements from politicians criticising the articles are painfully slow in coming reveals the lack of understanding in society.

Fortunately, several websites, including www.gay.lt and www.gayline.lt, keep the community together. There is one gay club in Vilnius. Until very recently, its regularly alternating locations had to be kept a tightly guarded secret. Now, however, there is a permanent address.

Men's Factory Ševčenkos 16; ✆ (8) 699-85009; www.gayclub.lt
Despite its rather seedy location down an inconspicuous back street a 10-min hike from the Old Town, Men's Factory finally has a fixed abode. The club is modestly sized, but that means it gets tightly packed, especially on the regularly scheduled events nights. Also on the menu are lasers, DJs, stage shows, snow machines and 'sweet surprises'. *Closed Sun–Tue.*

Shopping
SHOPPING CENTRES

The out-of-town shopping centre **Akropolis** on Ozo Street [*Vilnius* map], which opened in 2002 and which is expanding all the time, has excited Lithuanians and travellers from neighbouring countries too. Its website www.akropolis.lt details every shop there and all the entertainment available. For tourists it offers choice, space, cleanliness, extensive opening hours and heating or air conditioning as required. For souvenirs and books, prices are similar to those in the town. For alcohol, clothes and fabrics, they are much cheaper.

Visitors who knew the Soviet Union will find a trip to Akropolis a totally unreal experience and others who avoid such centres in the West may like to see how they can present a tasteful shopping environment. Families will be able to take advantage of the play areas and perhaps even the enormous ice-rink or bowling alley. One cannot imagine any hoodies here.

A smaller shopping centre, and one much more convenient for visitors staying in central Vilnius, is **Europa** (*Konstitucijos 7a; www.europa.lt*) which is opposite the Reval Lietuva and Best Western hotels. The shops all stay open until 22.00 (20.00 at weekends) and the restaurants until 24.00. Pre-booked groups can take the lift to the top of the Europa tower during the week and catering can be arranged there by any of the restaurants based in the complex, which means there is a wide choice. Individuals can go at any time (free of charge) at weekends between 10.00 and

24.00. Sunset is probably the best time for views, when the weather is good. The tower is 148m high, which makes it the tallest commercial building in the Baltics, although several churches in Tallinn and Riga still 'dwarf' it.

Visitors from other EU countries may want to take advantage of the low prices for vodka and fruit liqueurs charged in Vilnius, and which are lower in town than at the airport. There is now little restriction on the quantities brought back to the UK, as long as they are for personal use.

Bargaining may sometimes be possible in markets, but it will not reduce prices greatly and it is unlikely to be effective in shops. In the summer, visitors can expect shops that are relevant for tourists to be open seven days a week, except for the bookshops that still firmly close on Sundays. They will usually open at 10.00 and close at 19.00, although earlier closing times at the weekend are still quite common.

AMBER

Amber Aušros Vartų 9; ℩ (5) 212 1988
One of the most exclusive and expensive of the Old Town's little shops dealing in amber articles.

Amber Museum Gallery Šv Mykolo 8; ℩ (5) 262 3092 [2 G3]
Your necessary first stop if you want to know anything about amber, as well as buy genuine, beautifully crafted examples as jewellery or ornaments, this stylish little gallery has an enthusiastic and helpful English-speaking staff.

Amber

Lino-Gintaras Studija Didžioji 10; ☎ (5) 261 0213

Several branches of the 'Linen and Amber Studio' have popped up around the Old Town, others being at Stiklių 3 and Didžioji 5 and 6. They don't all sell precisely the same artefacts, some objects being highly artistic, others verging on the kitsch, so it is worth visiting each shop.

BOOKSHOPS

Akademinė Knyga Universiteto 4; ☎ (5) 261 9711

Close to the university, this stocks mainly reference books and academic literature, but also has a good stock of imported paperbacks.

Draugystė Gedimino 2; ☎ (5) 268 5081

The 'Friendship' bookstore has tomes in different languages, including coffee-table books and guidebooks.

Humanitas Vokiečių 2; ☎ (5) 262 1153

Venture to the far side of this exhibition hall of paintings and ceramics by Lithuanian artists and you'll discover the city's best selection of English-language art books.

Librairie Française Didžioji 1; ☎ (5) 262 0517; www.masiulis.lt

The Masiulio family who run this shop have been in the book trade since 1905, when they opened their first shop in Panevėžys. This was when it again became legal to sell books in the Lithuanian language using the Roman alphabet. Previously the family had to be smugglers, selling books printed in east Prussia and brought precariously across the

Nemunas River. Censorship would of course dog their work through much of the 20th century, although the original shop never actually closed. The family now run bookshops in each of the major towns in Lithuania. Despite the name, this shop actually has a good selection of books about Vilnius and Lithuania in English as well as in French. Those published abroad are often cheaper here than in Britain or in France. Visitors who read French can find an enormous selection of books on Napoleon and also on Marie Trintignant, the famous French actress murdered in Vilnius in July 2003 by her partner. She had been making a film in the university precincts about the French writer Colette.

Note the plaque on the wall outside commemorating Stendhal, the French writer who came to Vilnius in 1812.

Littera Universiteto 4; ☏ (5) 268 7258
With its elaborate frescoed interior, the bookshop within the university complex is undoubtedly the most attractive in the city and is worth a visit just to see this. The university T-shirts that it sells are tasteful and it is probably the only shop in Vilnius that sells attractive posters. It has a decent representation of English-language books about Lithuania. This is also the best place to obtain copies of the English-language literary magazine *Vilnius*. On the minus side, the staff are rude, the stock is chaotic and the lighting is poor.

Vaga Gedimino 50; ☏ (5) 249 8392
One of the longest-running bookstores in Vilnius. Stationery and cassettes are also on sale. English-language books are found in a room at the back of the top floor. A mezzanine sells pop and classical music CDs.

SOUVENIRS

Aukso Avis Savičiaus 8; ↘ (5) 261 0421
The best of Lithuanian textile art.

Maldis Basanavičiaus 4a; www.maldis.lt
Pricey antiques and artwork, some of which you can fit in your suitcase.

Mes Esame ('We Are') Pilies 42
This is a shop where articles produced by the disabled are sold. It is impossible to tell from the quality and quantity of materials and designs seen here. There are clothes, toys, ornaments and jewellery. It deserves support.

Rūta's Gallery Vokiečių 28; ↘ (8) 685 58415
Discover rich ceramic art, offbeat paintings, fascinating ornaments and handmade jewellery, all to the sound of relaxing, atmospheric music.

Sauluva Literatų 3; www.sauluva.lt
Housed in a fine old courtyard, this is the largest souvenir shop in Vilnius, selling ceramics, glassware, woodcarvings, leather goods and many other traditional artefacts, including candle houses which are made to order. It can therefore be seen as a one-stop shop for visitors who hate shopping, but feel obliged to do it.

Thelonius Stiklių 12; ↘ (5) 212 1076
For those small enough to manage to crawl down into this basement, there is a reward of a very wide selection of mostly jazz music, from both the Baltics area and further afield.

Verpstė Žydų 2; ☏ 262 5887
An odd, tiny gallery filled with gift and souvenir ideas in wood, ceramics, amber and linen, but irritatingly closed on Sun, Mon and other odd times.

Yzzy Gaono 10; www.yzzy.lt
The latest in Lithuanian designer clothes.

Monument to Grand Duke Gediminas

Souvenirs

⑨ Walking tours

Since the Old Town is one of the biggest and most beautiful in Europe, tourists tend to concentrate on the sights and attractions inside it. But the surrounding streets, hills and views offer a great deal too. While the main sights in the Old Town can be covered in one day, more time is needed for venturing beyond it. A route for a day-long walking tour is suggested below, followed by a few shorter ones.

OLD TOWN WALK

Start at **Vilnius Cathedral** (Arkikatedra Bazilika), a classical structure at the northern edge of the Old Town that was once the site of a revered pagan temple (page 140 [2 F2]). The first Christian church was probably built here following the Grand Duchy's initial conversion to Christianity in the 13th century, but most of what you see today dates from around 200 years ago. After Lithuania was occupied by Soviet forces, the three statues of saints that tower over the façade were removed and destroyed, only to be replaced by reproductions of the originals in 1996.

Inside, the impression is of an ornate gallery with oil paintings hung on two tiers, so it should come as no surprise to learn that the building was given the function of art gallery and concert hall under the Soviets. In the first decade after the war it was a garage for truck repairs.

One of the most resplendent of the 11 small chapels is also the oldest, the early 17th-century Baroque Chapel of St Casimir, patron saint of Vilnius. A visit to the

CROOKED CASTLE

From the top of the Higher Castle you can make out the white statue of three crosses on the adjacent hill. The Hill of Three Crosses was once the site of the Crooked Castle, a massive but vulnerable structure made of timber, clay, moss, mud and stone. It was built in the 14th century to house 4,000 soldiers and defend the town against the Bible-bashing Teutonic Order from the west. It had strong fortifications, but was easy to burn.

Grand Duke Jogaila converted to Christianity in 1386, but four years later the Crusaders returned to besiege Vilnius together with the forces of Vytautas the Great. It is believed that Jogaila's brother was brutally murdered in the Crooked Castle. When Jogaila and Vytautas forged an alliance in 1392 in which Vytautas became Grand Duke of Lithuania, the Teutonic Knights marched on Vilnius, stationed themselves in the Crooked Castle ruins and bombarded the Higher Castle across the narrow Vilnia valley day and night. English, French, Italian and Livonian soldiers beefed up the numbers of the attacking force, yet the Lithuanians still managed to withstand the assault and fight them off. By this time, there was nothing left of the Crooked Castle.

Old Town walk

vaults below reveals an altar once used for pagan rituals and the coffins of royal and noble family members whose lives have become romanticised among Lithuanians. Outside the cathedral, the **Clock Tower** (Arkikatedros varpinė), a favourite local rendezvous point, recently got a set of new bells that were blessed by Lithuania's Cardinal Bačkis before they were hung. The tower has a curious history. Its round lower storey, which is pierced by numerous gunports, dates back to the 14th century and belonged to the fortification system of the Lower Castle; it is the only part of it which survives to this day. It was converted into the cathedral's bell tower in the 1520s by the addition of two octagonal tiers. Later a fourth tier was added to house a clock, which still preserves its original mechanism. In 1893, it finally assumed its current appearance when it was crowned with a small steeple.

With your back to the cathedral doors, turn left and head across **Cathedral Square** (Katedros aikštė), a vast paved space to the side of the cathedral that makes an ideal starting or finishing point for parades and processions, towards the trees of Kalnų Park. But before you do so, search for the 'miracle stone'. It is said that here in Cathedral Square you can make your dreams come true by finding the slab marked *stebuklas* (miracle), then quickly making a wish while turning 360 degrees clockwise. This paving stone marks the end of the human chain that linked Tallinn, Riga, and Vilnius in 1989, formed by two million Lithuanians, Latvians and Estonians to protest against the Soviet occupation. However, you have to look for the mythical slab yourself, for superstition decrees that no one is allowed to reveal its precise location.

Since 1996, Cathedral Square has been the setting for a monument to Grand Duke Gediminas – a particularly fitting location, as it must be close to the spot where he had his legendary dream about the iron wolf. The commission for the statue was entrusted to veteran sculptor Vytautas Kašuba, who had spent most of his career in America and died soon after the monument was erected. Gediminas is shown with his sword in his left hand, an allusion to his supposed preference for diplomacy over war – though in reality he most probably used both to achieve substantial territorial gains for the Grand Duchy.

Being joint Capital of Culture in 2009 is bound to increase the amount of restoration work undertaken before that year. Immediately behind the cathedral is the most ambitious of these projects, the reconstruction of the Renaissance-style Royal Palace. A splendid medieval complex that fell into ruin and was finally destroyed by the Tsarist authorities in 1802, the aim is to complete the rebuilding by 2009 – also the date of Vilnius's momentous 1,000th anniversary.

Once inside tree-shaded Kalnų Park, keep left to find the path that winds upwards around the hill to the **Higher Castle** (Aukštutinės pilies bokštas), also known as Gedimino Castle, from which the best of the many views of Vilnius can be had (page 132 [2 G2]). The viewing platform at the top is worth the struggle to climb steps that are unnervingly narrow at times. The castle also houses a small museum of armoury and a model of medieval Vilnius.

Opened in 2005, a funicular railway leads back down to city level and the spacious courtyard of the **Applied Arts Museum** (Taikomosios dailės muziejus, page 130 [2 H1]). Enter either this or the **National Museum** (Lietuvos nacionalinis muziejus) from the front by first going through one of the gateways (page 136). A stylised statue of Mindaugas guarding the museum entrance was unveiled together with the King Mindaugas Bridge across the road to great fanfare and fireworks in July 2003, marking the 750th anniversary of the coronation that brought Christianity to Vilnius for the first time.

Head back past the front of the Cathedral, diagonally across Cathedral Square, and find the northern end of Pilies, the Old Town's mainly pedestrian-only thoroughfare. A handful of cafés here make a convenient pause for breath and sell good coffee, cakes, lunches and ice cream. Take Bernadinų, the first narrow lane to the left, which snakes past the **Adam Mickiewicz Museum** (Mickevičiaus butas-muziejus, page 136 [2 G3]) towards **St Anne's Church** (Šv Onos bažnyčia), the charming Gothic church that Napoleon famously said he would like to take back to Paris on the palm of his hand (page 144 [2 H3]). The more imposing **Bernadine Church** (Bernadinų bažnyčia) stands immediately behind it (page 146 [2 H3]).

Double back across busy Maironio Street to find **St Michael's Church** (Šv Mykolo bažnyčia) [2 H3], which since the Soviet period has housed the Museum of Architecture, interesting as a

St Michael's Church

curiosity since it displays plans of buildings in Vilnius that were never approved. Built by the head of one of Vilnius's great noble families, Leonas Sapiega, as a personal mausoleum in the early 1600s, one or two of the church's lovely details, like the rosette ceiling, are also worth popping in for. Further along Šv Mykolo is the **Amber Museum-Gallery** (Gintaro muziejus-galerija), Vilnius's most illuminating museum (and shop) dedicated exclusively to Baltic Gold (page 130 [2 G3]).

The street brings you back onto bustling Pilies. Turn left and walk up, pausing at Pilies 26. Known today as the **Signatories' House** (Signatarų namai) [2 G3], this was where the 20 members of the Council of Lithuania met in 1918 to sign a declaration on the nation's independence. There is not a great deal in this small museum to see – only to imagine. Even the declaration itself is not on show. It has disappeared, since in Polish and Soviet times it needed to be hidden, and there are various theories as to where it might be. One theory doing the rounds in 2005 was that it might be hidden in the walls of the Lithuanian Language Institute on Antakalnio, near SS Peter and Paul Church. In 1918 the house belonged to a rich architect Petras Vileisis whose brother Jonas was one of the signatories. Jonas may have taken the document to him and for safekeeping hidden it within a wall. The first and ground floors of the museum both have exhibition rooms where temporary artistic and photographic displays are held.

Stroll through the arcade over the road to browse through thousands of souvenirs, classier and pricier versions of which are on display in several amber and linen shops along this part of the street. At the top of the arcade, Pilies opens out onto more stalls selling everything from gimmicky ceramics to woolly socks. A lovely row of shops on the left includes a charity shop selling stuffed toys and knick-knacks handmade by the disabled, a tea shop, a gallery showcasing local artists and an irresistible attraction for choc-lovers – a shop with a bounteous display of chocolates of every size, shape and filling. Venture a little further into Bokšto to find the city's eclectic Russian and, round the corner, Polish art galleries.

The downstairs section of the **Šlapelis Museum** at Pilies 40 [2 G4] is a re-creation of the pioneering Lithuanian bookshop established in 1906 by Jurgis Šlapelis and his wife Marija. Displayed in the couple's flat above, which is entered from the courtyard, are books and other objects associated with the national cultural revival they did so much to promote, as well as exhibits from the little-documented inter-war Polish period.

Over the square, standing on a platform above an open-air art market, is **St Paraskeva Russian Orthodox Church** (Piatnickaya cerkvė), originally built in 1345, where Peter the Great of Russia supposedly stood as godfather to the christening of Hannibal, the great grandfather of the Russian poet Alexander Pushkin in 1705. Hannibal was abducted from his home in Africa at the age of seven, rescued from his life as a slave in Istanbul by the Russian envoy and presented as a gift to Tsar Peter.

As the road upwards closes in to become Didžioji, **Vilnius Picture Gallery** (Vilniaus paveikslų galerija) lies beyond an unassuming gateway on the left that leads into a grand and elegant courtyard (page 139 [2 G4]). Another of the city's Russian

Orthodox churches, the Byzantine-style **St Nicolas** (Šv Mikalojaus cerkvė) [2 G4], an oasis of candlelit peace away from the bustle of the street, can be explored a short distance further up Didžioji on the left. As with all of Vilnius's Russian Orthodox churches, no concessions are made to Lithuania; everything is written, spoken and sung in Russian.

As Didžioji broadens enough to deserve its name ('great'), boutiques on both sides reveal how many of the Western world's fashion brands are on offer in today's transformed Vilnius. But to discover how most of the city's churches looked 20 years ago, forlorn, dilapidated and empty, take the first street left, Savičiaus. About 100m down on the right is **St Mary the Soothing** (Marijos Ramintojos bažnyčia) [4 G5], its courtyard locked and unkempt. The single tower of this late Baroque church dates from the mid-18th century and is still tall enough to feature as part of the Vilnius skyline.

Double back to Didžioji, passing the **M K Čiurlionis House** (M K Čiurlionio namai) dedicated to Lithuania's most beloved artist and composer (page 133 [4 G5]). Another essential museum for art-lovers can be found at number 26. The astonishing legacy of an artist who returned to his home country from America in 1998, the **Kazys Varnelis House Museum** contains an astonishing personal collection of art (page 139 [4 F5]). Cross the street to the grand, 18th-century **Town Hall** (Rotušė) [4 F5], which today has multiple uses, ranging from classical music venue to contemporary art gallery. The foyer makes an austere setting for often absorbing exhibitions of art and architecture.

Keep heading upwards, bearing left of the town hall, and after a few steps **St Casimir's** (Šv Kazimiero bažnyčia) comes into view. This was Vilnius's very first Baroque building, modelled on Rome's church of Il Gesu with the characteristically Lithuanian addition of twin spires (page 146 [4 G5]). Occupying powers have done some odd things with St Casimir's. During the six months Napoleon was in control of Vilnius the church stored wine for the French army. It was during the Nazi occupation in 1942 that St Casimir's royal lineage was recognised by placing a gold-coloured crown above the central dome. Then, in the Soviet period, St Casimir's became the city's museum of atheism.

An intersection of streets appears further up the hill, with a small parking area in front of the **National Philharmonic** (Filharmonija). Take a peek down charmingly narrow Šv Kazimiero Street, which dips back to the left, before approaching Aušros Vartų with its myriad of churches, spires and souvenir shops (seek out the bizarre and cluttered workshop of local craftsman Jonas Bugailiškis at number 17). What immediately catches your eye is the stunning 18m-high Baroque **Basilian Gate** (Bazilijonų vartai). It leads to a monastery that is used by a small group of Uniate Basilian monks and its rundown **Church of the Holy Trinity** (Šv Trejybės cerkvė). Wander beyond the gateway to discover the church and the monastery's calm courtyard. The monastery served as a conveniently isolated prison in Tsarist times and the poet Adam Mickiewicz was held here for a while, a fact recorded on a plaque. Restoration of the church and its 16th-century frescoes is expected to take many years. Another peaceful, leafy courtyard next to the curious **Arka Art Gallery** (Arka galerija), immediately before the Basilian Gate, is a relaxing coffee stop served by the Arka café.

Aušros Vartų now takes in the Orthodox **Church of the Holy Spirit** (Šv Dvasios cerkvė), the most revered religious building of Lithuania's Russian-speaking community, found through another gateway (page 148 [4 G6]). The forms of what is said to be the miraculously preserved bodies of saints Anthony, Ivan and Eustace, who died for their faith in 1347, can still be seen underneath their shrouds. They were murdered by militant pagans on the spot where the Church of the Holy Trinity now stands. At the far end of Aušros Vartų, beyond **St Teresa's Church** (Šv Teresės bažnyčia) [4 G7], lies the climax to this pilgrimage between the spires of Vilnius, the **Gates of Dawn** (Aušros Vartų koplytėlė) [4 G7], to which the most pious of worshippers crawl in veneration up steps from street level. The gates hold a gold-and-silver image of the Virgin Mary in a chapel that is a shrine for devout Catholics.

Gates of Dawn

Backtrack down past the Philharmonic and take a left on Etmonų, at the end of which stand the Youth Theatre and Puppet Theatre. Both opened many years before independence but have found new audiences as Lithuanians keep up their passionate love of the stage (page 95 [4 F6]). Take the passage right, which brings you alongside the Radisson SAS to the rear of the town hall. Head left and left again onto Rūdininkų for two sites that bring back the tragedy of the Holocaust in Vilnius. This was then part of the terror-stricken 'ghetto' where the city's large Jewish population were kept before being herded out for extermination. A map on the wall of Rūdininkų 18, where one of the ghetto gates stood, shows how the streets looked at that time. A courtyard at Rūdininkų 8 was where the cruel process of selection was made. Jewish families were permitted only two children in the ghetto. If there were more, the parents had to choose who was to be taken away and killed. The old and weak – those of no practical use to the Nazis – were also 'selected' here. A plaque on the wall marks this terrible place.

Back on Vokiečių, a broad avenue that is home to more fashionable independent shops and boutiques, the **Contemporary Art Centre** (Šiolaikinio meno centras) holds some of the city's most daring modern artwork (page 133 [4 F5]). About 50m up Šv Mikalojaus, the second lane on the left, find the oldest Gothic building still standing in Vilnius, **St Nicholas's Church** (Šv Mikalojaus bažnyčia), built in 1320 to serve German merchants in the years before Lithuania itself widely adopted Christianity. When Lithuanians' cultural and religious activities were severely restricted during Poland's occupation of Vilnius between the wars, this was the only church where they were allowed to attend mass in their language.

In 2004, a new **Jewish Museum** was opened to the public at Naugarduko 10. Now called the Tolerance Centre (page 135 [3 C6]), gradually the collections at the other Jewish museums, at Pylimo 4 and Pamėnkalnio 12, are being transferred here. Some exhibits are moved over each year. If you visit one of these museums, it should be the 'green house' at Pamėnkalnio 12, set back up a hill from the main street. Here you'll find a chilling photographic record of sites where massacres under the Nazis took place. But all three museums stand as a ghostly reminder of what was once a thriving Jewish community. About 200 Jewish communities existed in Lithuania before World War II. Vilnius, where 40% of the population was Jewish, had 105 synagogues and prayer houses and six daily Jewish newspapers, making Vilna, as it was known in Yiddish, the 'Jerusalem of the North'. About 300,000 Jews lived in Lithuania at the turn of the last century. More than 90% of this community was wiped out during the Nazi occupation.

An appropriate few hundred metres away from these memorials to tragedy is Vilnius's strangest statue. It is of the late Californian rock musician **Frank Zappa**, but was in fact unveiled in 1995, two years after his death. He had hoped to visit Lithuania to see it but his final illness prevented this. Find it by turning off Pylimo up Kalinausko; it is in a rather mediocre courtyard behind the first office block on the right. It is probably a suitable compromise for its location. Those who see statutes as a way of the establishment perpetuating itself for ever will probably not be aware of it, and those with a sense of humour will be relieved that the ultimate figure of anti-establishment behaviour will not be forgotten.

Return to Vokiečių via Vilniaus, passing the **Theatre, Music & Film Museum** on your right [1 D4]. The first courtyard on the right after Trakų reveals the location of one of Vilnius's newest and most colourful art shops, **Rūta's Gallery** (Rūtos galerija), whose imaginatively styled paintings, sculptures, dishes, handmade jewellery and other items are reasonably priced and not too bulky to take home (page 106 [3 C8]). Another easily missed courtyard at Vokiečių 20 leads to a church that has served Vilnius's Lutheran community since 1555, known today as the **Evangelical Lutheran Church** (Evangelikų Liuteronų bažnyčia). The main point of interest here is the elaborate Rococo altar, built in 1741 by the same architect who designed the magnificent Basilian Gate and the Orthodox Church of the Holy Spirit, Jan Krzysztof Glaubitz. The stunning ornateness of the altar stands out boldly against the whitewashed interior.

Cross to the other side of Vokiečių, doubling back slightly, and dive through one of the archways beneath the residential buildings into a broad courtyard to find the tail-end of Žydų (Jews') Street. This is where the Great Synagogue, the centrepiece of Vilnius's thriving Jewish community, stood before it was badly bombed during the war and finally destroyed completely in the early years of the Soviet occupation to make way for a school. A small monument to the Talmudic scholar Rabbi Elijah, the Vilna Gaon, stands at the back of the school, solitarily lamenting a lost world of 300,000 Jews who lived and worked in confined, cobbled streets that stretched like a maze through this part the Old Town.

Žydų emerges onto the similarly narrow Stiklių, which has an array of poky gift and clothes shops both left and right. Pause for a well-deserved coffee, cake or lunch break at Ponių Laimė on the corner. The tour heads left from Žydų down Stiklių to reach Domininkonų. The focal point for the city's Polish faithful is the cavernous **Church of the Holy Spirit** (Šventosios Dvasios bažnyčia), a few steps to the left (page 147 [1 E4]), while down the hill on the right, on Universiteto, lies the charming complex of courtyards that makes up **Vilnius University** (Vilniaus Universitetas). Before exploring this, however, pop into one of the city's most beautiful Baroque courtyards, at Universiteto 2. In summer this is the gorgeous backdrop to the Sole Luna café and makes a wonderful location for a daytime coffee and crêpe or an evening beer.

Vilnius University (page 156 [2 F3]) dates back more than 400 years, although the city's history as victim of persecution and occupation ensured that it did not stay open all that time. The Russians closed it in 1832 and it wasn't until 1919, the year after Lithuania won its long-awaited independence, that it reopened. There are 12 courtyards to discover, some more tricky to find than others. Try to visualise the map at Universiteto 7 before entering. In the grand courtyard at the top of the steps is the monumental façade of **St John's Church** (Šv Jono bažnyčia), beyond which lies a magnificent interior and intimidating assemblage of ten altars (page 149 [2 F3]).

Exit the university where you came in and, opposite, find the **President's Palace** (L R Prezidentūra) [2 F3], a building with a history dating back to the 14th century and where Napoleon slept in 1812 on his doomed march to Moscow. Today, after many renovations, it houses the busy offices of the Lithuanian president. It is open on Fridays and Saturdays for pre-booked groups. A tour showing the main reception rooms, the President's Office and the gardens takes about 45 minutes. The furnishings are entirely modern, much of them in oak and birch, but the designs

Old Town walk

are from the early 19th century. One room has four large portraits of the previous Lithuanian presidents, three from the 1920–40 period and one of Algirdas Brazauskas, in office 1993–98. An even larger painting shows Vytautas the Great riding into the Black Sea, recalling the time when the Polish-Lithuanian Commonwealth stretched that far in the mid-15th century.

FURTHER WALKS
Changing Vilnius walk

Of course, there's more to Vilnius than the Old Town. Gedimino Avenue is the city's main drag, extending westwards from the cathedral. It is lined with ever-increasing numbers of classy shops, apartments and mini-malls. Real estate developers are sure that Gedimino will quickly become one long, highly attractive, open-air shopping centre to rival anything Copenhagen or London have to offer. That's ambitious. But with the avenue now physically transformed all the way to the Žvėrynas suburb in the west, the paving evened, underground parking installed and the groaning trolleybuses banished to just one intersection, they are not so far off the mark.

Changes are visible right the way along the street. The Vilnius municipality offices have moved from Gedimino 9 to a new skyscraper the other side of the river, leaving this neo-Baroque block to re-emerge as a swanky superstore; one of the city's grimy old cinemas has become a Benetton store; the towering Novotel is a brand new building with fashion shops on the ground floor; and the 19th-century building at Gedimino 20, once the shabby Hotel Vilnius, shines like never before as the multi-million pound commercial and residential Grand Duke Palace.

The most essential thing to see on Gedimino Avenue, however, has stayed structurally unchanged since it was built as a courthouse and prison in 1899. Now housing the vivid and shocking basement-level **KGB Museum** (Genocido aukų muziejus), the much-feared building facing **Lukiškių Square** was the Soviet secret service's Vilnius headquarters (page 135 [*Vilnius* map]). Hundreds of people were imprisoned, tortured and executed in its cells and thousands more were sent to Siberia between the 1940s and the 1980s.

In the middle of the square a giant statue of Lenin gestured with arm outstretched at the KGB building. It was pulled apart by a crane in front of cheering crowds in 1991 and now stands at the Grutas Park of Soviet Statues near Druskininkai.

Gedimino extends beyond the Lithuanian Music Academy, where free public concerts are frequently held in term time, to its westernmost section, which boasts even more boutiques and independent shops. Concealed from view, one of the country's biggest prisons lurks down Ankštoji, a narrow side street to the right.

Before reaching the River Neris, the avenue opens out into **Independence Square** (Nepriklausomybės aikštė), bordered on one side by the 'Stalinist Baroque' **National Library** (Martynas Mažvydas biblioteka), built in the 1950s, and on the other by the late Soviet-era **Parliament** building (Seimas), which originally housed the Supreme Council of Lithuania. This is where the republic's leaders declared independence from Moscow on 11 March 1990. Barricades were erected to

Further walks

protect the Parliament from Soviet tanks. These giant cubes and slabs of crude concrete remained in place into the early 1990s. Today, a few can still be seen on the side of the building facing the river.

Stroll across the recently renovated old river-bridge into the leafy residential district of Žvėrynas to find the eye-catching onion domes of the Russian Orthodox **Church of the Apparition of the Holy Mother of God** (Znamenskaya cerkvė), one of the city's warmest and most appealing churches. As Žvėrynas quickly became the city's first garden suburb, divided into separate plots in the 1890s, this was the first church to be built here, in 1903. To the left, where Vytauto meets Liubarto, and a little to the right stands the tiny, Moorish-style **Kenessa**, built for the Karaite community in 1922, but used as a warehouse during the Soviet occupation.

Žvėrynas, a dense knit of streets, some of them almost rustic with quaint wooden houses, is arranged in a bend in the river. It is an increasingly chic place to live, no more than a square mile wide and very pleasant to stroll around. Find the suspension bridge dramatically spanning the river from grassy banks into the tall pines of Vingis Park on the far side.

Bohemian Vilnius walk

The **Hill of Three Crosses** (Trijų kryžių kalnas) is another of Vilnius's dramatic viewpoints, higher than the castle, from which the entire panorama of the Old Town is visible. Reach it via an open-air stadium from the southern end of T.Kosciuškos, or cross a wooden bridge over the Vilnia from tennis courts in Sereikiškių Park and follow the river to the right before finding steep and rickety steps to the top.

The Hill of Three Crosses

The gleaming white crosses are a replacement for wooden crosses first raised here 350 years ago commemorating 14 monks who were dragged from a Vilnius monastery in the 14th century and murdered by pagans. Seven of them were butchered in cold blood, the rest tied to crosses and floated down the River Neris. The crosses were removed by the Soviets in 1950.

Sereikiškių Park borders Užupis, another quietly charming part of the city to stroll about. But it has a wacky side too. Užupis is the equivalent of Greenwich Village in New York or Montmartre in Paris, a place with unconventional ideals and creativity. It declared itself the 'breakaway republic of Užupis' in 1998, with its own independence day on 1 April, its own **constitution**, which is nailed to the wall on Paupio Street, and its own flag, president and customs officers – who always seem to be off duty. Its 'national symbol', an **angel** blowing her horn in celebration of freedom and independence, stands atop a column in the central square. The names of everyone who contributed the cash to make it are carved into the base.

Užupis literally means 'the other side of the river'. Up until a decade ago this was one of the most neglected and squalid areas in Vilnius, populated by drunks and criminal types. Today it is prime real estate. Parts are still ruinously rundown, but it is a fascinating place to wander. It might remind you of small towns in Italy, with its smattering of outdoor cafés and boys and girls roaring about on mopeds.

To enter Užupis, pass the white-box **Church of the Holy Mother of God** – a Russian Orthodox church that has over the years been a barracks, a library, a university department and a smithy – cross the bubbling Vilnia into Užupio Street. The building with the welcoming terrace just across the water is the Užupio Café, frequented by artists, poets, and all manner of bohemians. As you cross the bridge, look down at the wall of the near bank to see the Užupis Mermaid, a beautiful little siren who bids adieu to visitors leaving the Old Town.

After the café, at the end of a little alley to the left, is the **Alternative Art Centre**, worth a look for its bizarre 'art' collection. Retrace your steps and just a little up the street at number 5 is the **Užupio Gallery**, a working gallery that features unique enamel items and jewellery.

Užupis is full of lovely courtyards. Don't be afraid to poke your head in and look around. As you face the angel from its front, enter the archway on the right and you will feel as if you've stepped back in time. Notice the water pump, which supplies water for washing dishes and clothes, and for drinking.

Climb the hill and bear right at the fork (bear left to find Tores, the bar and restaurant with the best terrace view in town). Pass the unmarked morgue on the left. When you reach a bus stop and an old payphone, turn right onto Žvirgždyno Street, marked by a small, rusty sign. Fifty metres ahead is the entrance to the **Bernardine Cemetery** (Bernardinų kapinės), one of the most serene and beautiful places in Vilnius. It was founded in 1810 by Bernardine monks and stands on the tall banks of the Vilnia, virtually undisturbed by visitors. University professors, artists and scientists are among the people laid to rest here.

21st-century Vilnius walk

Having had foreign monuments stamped all over its streets and squares in the past, Vilnius seems wary of erecting new ones to the grand dukes of its illustrious history or to the national heroes of its fight for survival. But monuments to capitalism, each more impressive than the last, are rising all the time. The riverbank between the southern end of A.Goštauto and the precarious, two-lane Geležinio Vilko is known today as the Business Triangle, crammed with flashy new high-rise office buildings. Close by, the Vilnius Gates (Vilniaus vartai), opened in 2006, tower above the Geležinio Vilko underpass.

However, the most visually striking of all these post-millennium skyscraper projects is **Europa Square** (Europos aikštė) and the sleek, glass-fronted structures around it. The wall of windows facing recently renamed Konstitucijos (Constitution) Avenue is the new **City Hall**, inside which is an accessible ground-floor room displaying a fascinating model of all the future construction developments in Vilnius. Behind it, at 134 metres, the circular **Europa Tower** (Europos bokštas) is the Baltic countries' tallest building. Thirty-three floors up, the panorama of Vilnius from the viewing platform is unrivalled – and it's free to get to the top. Just enter the ground floor and ask the security guard. But attempt this only at weekends; the companies that rent these prestigious offices do not want nosy sightseers getting lost or clogging up the elevators.

Arguably the most comfortable view in Vilnius, however, is from one of the curvaceous, ocean-blue chairs of the 22nd-floor **SkyBar** in the Reval Hotel Lietuva, just across Konstitucijos Avenue from Europa Square. Sitting with cocktail in hand, this is a perfect spot to watch the sunset.

Before 2002, these streets north of the river were a no-go area for most tourists, a scruffy mess of Soviet-era concrete, home to a few straggly shops and a shopping centre that more resembled an indoor market selling clothes, watches and electrical gadgets that had fallen off the backs of trucks.

Much of the ugly concrete is still there. But squeaky clean, colourfully landscaped shopping centres filled with refreshing air conditioning and the sound of running water – in particular the **Central Universal Store** (VCUP) and the **Europa Shopping Centre** – are taking the attention away from the eyesores. The latter include the pedestrian precinct between the refurbished Reval and the Green Bridge, once a futuristic showpiece of the late communist years. Now it is crumbling and cracked and permeated by strip bars. Halfway down the precinct, the **Planetarium** is still operational, despite having a furniture showroom in the lobby.

The **Green Bridge** (Žaliasis tiltas) itself is firmly part of the old era, its comical Socialist Realist figures of grim workers and determined peasants a bizarre contrast to the skyscrapers behind it. Why they were not pulled down immediately after the collapse of the Soviet Union, along with Lenin, and deported to the Grutas Soviet theme park is a matter of intense speculation. The authorities say that they stand as a warning to future generations of the horrors (artistic and otherwise) of communist rule. But it is also true that many locals actually see them as genuine works of art, created by Lithuanian sculptors, not imported from Moscow. In a similar way, many residents are proud, not ashamed, of architectural monsters such as the gargantuan **Opera and Ballet Theatre** (Operos ir baletos teatras), which virtually overshadows the Green Bridge, or the Parliament building, or even the city's hideous high-rise suburbs, all of which were designed by Lithuanian architects.

The green swathe of riverbank west of the Green Bridge is gradually being put to use. Next to the pedestrian-only **White Bridge** (Baltasis tiltas), which daredevil stunt pilot Jurgis Kairys flew under in 1999, are skateboarding, basketball and volleyball courts for restless youths – and '**The Beach**'. In summer, sip on a cold local draught beer under imported palm trees as the sand, brought here in trucks all the way from Lithuania's coastal dunes, tickles your toes.

10 Museums and sightseeing

MUSEUMS AND GALLERIES

In an irritating overhang from earlier times, most museums are closed on at least one day a week – usually Sunday or Monday – and many for two days; they also close on public holidays. Most do not open until 10.00 and rare is the museum that closes as late as 18.00. Churches are open every day from around 09.00.

Admission prices here are given for adults. Most museums give reductions for children, senior citizens and, providing you have an international card, students and teachers. The websites www.muziejai.lt and www.lnm.lt provide further information.

Amber Museum-Gallery Šv Mykolo 8; ☎ 262 3092 [2 G3]
Open 10.00–19.00. Free admission.
Privately run (it's a shop too), this gallery reveals the history of Baltic gold in several cavernous cellar rooms. You can also find amber here at the gallery in blue, black, white, red and green. It has plenty of unusual, handmade items to choose from including exquisitely designed necklaces, miniature amber musical instruments, even an amber-coloured liqueur in a flask with amber-topped stopper. Each piece comes with a certificate of authenticity.

Applied Arts Museum Arsenalo 3a; ☎ 262 8080 [2 H1]
Open Tue–Sat 11.00–17.30, Sun 11.00–15.30. Admission 6Lt.
Constructed as an arsenal in the 16th century by Sigismund the Old, the more

decorative third floor being added by his son a few decades later, this was at the time the biggest building in the Polish-Lithuanian Commonwealth. It was virtually destroyed when the Russians invaded and pillaged the city in 1655, only to be rebuilt 150 years later.

These days it houses a rather austere collection of portraits, but also one or two paintings that are worth the price of admission alone, including canvases by Francisco Ximenez, Luis Morales and the master of Austrian Baroque, Johann Michael Rottmayr. Don't miss also one of the best displays of folk art and Lithuanian wooden crosses. Many of these are by Vincas Svirkis (1835–1916), who spent his life roaming the countryside carving saints and religious scenes into the crosses he left behind as he moved from village to village.

Artillery Bastion Bokšto 20; ☎ 261 2149 [4 H6]
Open 10.00–18.00 except Sun–Mon. Admission 2Lt.
In centuries past, this part of Vilnius was infamous for its prostitution and wild taverns. Witches were said to gather here for demonic orgies. The bastion, part of the city's 17th-century defence against invading armies of Russians and Swedes, quickly fell into ruin and was used in the 19th century as a windowless orphanage, then became a rat-infested rubbish dump and public lavatory. The Soviets used it to store vegetables until it was finally restored in 1967. Today, there is not a great deal to see beyond a handful of old cannons, but there is plenty of history to imagine in the darkness. The fat, round walls of the Subačiaus Gate, home to the Vilnius

Executioner, used to stand adjacent to the Bastion. With his mask on, he would walk down Subačiaus to Town Hall Square where condemned prisoners awaited their fate. The Slavs who tended to live on Subačiaus said that they knew the executioner's identity, because their dogs would bark at him, mask on or off.

Higher Castle Arsenalo 5; ☎ 261 7453 [2 G2]
Open 10.00–17.00 except Mon. Admission 4Lt.

A climb via cobbled path to the top of 50m-high Gediminas Hill rewards with a perfectly situated viewpoint across the rooftops and spires of the Old Town. A recently installed, super-smooth funicular railway, found in the courtyard of the Applied Arts Museum, makes the going easy up to this point. Take the natural next step and scramble to the summit – the viewing platform atop the Higher Castle – and the reward will be even greater.

Higher Castle

In this 180-degree panorama, it is possible to make out virtually every major landmark in Vilnius, from the Gothic spires of St Anne's Church in the east, to the new financial centre rising up from the grassy banks on the opposite side of the river. Vilnius's Soviet-era high-rise housing and Television Tower stand out among the trees on the horizon; if it were not for these, one would have the impression of a city surrounded on all sides by thick forest. As such, the Higher Castle makes an ideal place to begin or end a tour of the city. Normally, in summer, the best light for photography is in the later part of the day.

The museum housed in the castle shows models of the castles of Vilnius as they looked in the 14th and 17th centuries, as well as a display of weapons, armour and a few maps. Other than the tower, little remains of the castle save for the fragments of outer walls.

It can now be taken for granted that the Lithuanian flag will be raised on the castle tower every day. This first happened on 1 January 1919, but following the Polish seizure of Vilnius in 1920, it was not seen again here until 1939. The flag was banned again in 1944 when the Soviets established what seemed to be a permanent occupation, but was courageously raised once more on 7 October 1988, three years before their regime finally collapsed.

M K Čiurlionis Museum Savičiaus 11; ☏ 262 2451 [4 G5]
Open 10.00–16.00 except Sat–Sun. Free admission.
The grand piano on which the gifted Lithuanian composer and painter wrote some of his best pieces is the main object of interest here. Prolific and yet at the same time a sufferer of depression and insomnia, M K Čiurlionis (1875–1911) lived in this small apartment in 1907–08. Fans of his paintings, like the cycle on the signs of the zodiac, will have to travel to the far more interesting Čiurlionis Museum in Kaunas.

Contemporary Art Centre Vokiečių 2; ☏ 262 3476 [4 F5]
Open 12.00–21.00 except Mon. Admission 6Lt.

Museums and galleries

Right alongside the town hall stands the concrete-and-glass Contemporary Art Centre, which, although an ugly blot on the face of the Old Town, provides much-needed display space for exhibitions that are predominantly, but not exclusively, of the works of living artists. The shows here are usually highly original and often shocking. The gallery's single permanent display is on Fluxus, a bizarre experimental art movement led by the Lithuanian-born George Maciunas, friend of Yoko Ono and John Lennon, which thrived in the US in the 1960s.

Jewish Museum Paménkalnio 12; ℡ 262 0730 [1 C3]
Open Mon–Thu 09.00–17.00, Fri 09.00–16.00, Sun 10.00-16.00. Free admission.
The wooden 'green house' houses a documentary display focusing on Jewish culture and life in Vilnius and Lithuania immediately before World War II and its destruction during the Holocaust. Outside stands a monument entitled Moonlight, which commemorates Chiune Sugihara the Kaunas-based Japanese diplomat who is credited with rescuing up to 6,000 Jews, by granting them transit visas through Japan and therefore the opportunity to leave Lithuania.

Housed in a tenement building at Pylimo 4 is the Lithuanian State Jewish Museum, on the first floor of which are displays of liturgical objects, dolls used for theatrical performances during the Feast of Purim, prints and drawings of Vilnius's Great Synagogue, and photographs, supplemented by a few tantalising fragments, of the wonderfully elaborate wooden synagogues, all now destroyed, which once graced several Lithuanian towns. Two rooms on the floor above are dedicated to a photographic record of memorial sites throughout Lithuania to victims of Nazism, and to a gallery honouring those who sheltered or otherwise saved Jews.

The **Tolerance Centre** at Naugarduko 10 [3 C6] opened in 2004 and since then the collections found at Pylimo 4 and Pamėnkalnio 12 have been gradually transferred here.

KGB Museum Aukų 2a; ✆ 249 6264 [*Vilnius* map]
Open 10.00–17.00 except Mon. Admission 2Lt.

The entrance to one of Vilnius's most essential sites is at the western side of the building, as the front on the square is now a memorial to the many people who died there. In Soviet guidebooks, the building is described simply as 'a municipal institution'. In due course, it is intended to present a full documentary record on Soviet repression against Lithuania (particularly the Siberian deportations), and on the resistance to it. The first part of this exhibition opened in spring 2005.

In the mean time, the cells in the basement, which were used for the imprisonment and torture of political opponents until 1991, can be visited. These include an isolation cell which has neither heating nor windows, a special padded and soundproofed cell for suicide risks, and two cells where water torture was administered in order to keep prisoners constantly awake.

There is documentary material on some of the most prominent victims, while sacks of incriminating documents shredded by the KGB in the final three years of

Soviet rule are also on view. A former execution chamber opened to the public in 2003. Great efforts were made to conceal this activity from the other prisoners, including naming the area 'the kitchen' and delaying executions until the spring, when removal and burial of the bodies became easier.

There are short labels in good English throughout the museum, but it is certainly worth hiring the audio guide for a fuller explanation of the terrifying role this building played through the Soviet period in Lithuania. The ticket desk sells several books in English about repression at that time.

Adam Mickiewicz Museum Bernadinų 11; ℡ 279 1879 [2 G3]
Open Tue–Fri 10.00–17.00, Sat–Sun 10.00–14.00, closed Sun. Admission 2Lt.
The famous Polish poet lived here for only two months, in 1822, but this apartment-museum provides the best insight into his life and creative mind to be found in Vilnius. It also shows paintings and engravings that reveal something of everyday life in the city at that time. Poland's greatest national poet is also one of Lithuania's national heroes, as the first words of his best-known epic *Pan Tadeusz* make perfectly clear: 'Lithuania, my homeland, you are like health. Only he who has lost you can know how much you are cherished.'

National Museum Arsenalo 1; ℡ 262 9426
Open 10.00–18.00, except Mon–Tue. Admission 4Lt.
Curios as diverse as a wonderfully ornate Baroque-style sledge from the 18th century, a handprint in iron of Peter the Great made at the opening of a smelting

house in Belmontas, built to make guns for Russia's war against Sweden, and a Vilnius executioner's sword are just a few of the exhibits that brighten up the first hall. The sword, made in Germany in the early 17th century, is broken into two pieces, perhaps from a particularly tough neck. Exotic gifts from far and wide that have found their way here include a fan from the Emperor of Japan, presented to the officers of a Russian frigate in 1857, and an Egyptian sarcophagus that was a gift from the Museum of Prague in 1899.

Upstairs, a new exhibition celebrating Vilnius's millennial birthday in 2009 guides visitors through the history of Lithuania starting from 1,000 years ago. Fascinating maps, weapons, portraits, coins and other more unusual objects illustrate the battles against the Teutonic Order, the empire of the Grand Duchy, and everyday life in Vilnius in the centuries since then. The exhibition really emphasises the life of the citizens of Vilnius, the display showing satchels, plates, spoons, scarves and perfume bottles dating back to the 1600s. Another hall shows how rooms in typical Lithuanian farmsteads looked in centuries past. While large families often lived in cluttered surroundings, one room was always kept spotlessly clean in case visitors came to call unexpectedly. For an illuminating tour of the museum, ask for an English-speaking guide.

Pushkin Memorial Museum Subačiaus 124; ☎ 260 0080 [*Vilnius* map]
Open 10.00–17.00 except Mon–Tue. Admission 4Lt.
A hike along Subačiaus out to Vilnius's farthest reaches, or a ride on bus number

Museums and galleries

10 southwards from the cathedral, will take you through the shadowy residential district of Markučiai to a park and a hilltop house. The great Russian poet never lived here, of course, but his son Grigorij (1835–1905) did, together with his wife Varvara (1855–1935). Today, this large, rather rickety wooden house is home to many volumes of Pushkin's works and other curios, the ground floor furnished in the style of the late 19th century. Stroll to the back of the house, past a statue of Pushkin, and the quiet grounds extend to steps leading down to a lake. Paths reach out from here into the surrounding countryside and are a delight to explore.

Radvila Palace Vilniaus 22; ↘ 262 0981 [1 D3]
Open 12.00–17.00 except Mon. Admission 5Lt.
A generally austere collection of art from the 16th century onwards. Built for Jonušas Radvila, Voivod of Vilnius and Grand Hetman of Lithuania, this 17th-century Renaissance-style palace is now used mainly for showcasing 165 portrait engravings of Radvila family members, and also for the odd music concert.

Theatre, Music & Film Museum Vilniaus 41; ↘ 262 2406 [1 D4]
Open Tue–Fri 12.00–18.00, Sat 11.00–16.00. Admission 4Lt.
Despite its name, the 'display' on film is disappointingly cursory, with the briefest of looks at Lithuanian successes during the later Soviet years and virtually nothing on Lithuanian directors and actors since then. This history of the performing arts instead concentrates on the glory days before World War II, with keyboard instruments, still-working musical boxes and musty theatre costumes. One local theatre-turned-

cinema director explains his request for subsidies from the Lithuanian government with his idea that 'In future cultural life, films will take the place of the theatre.'

Kazys Varnelis House Museum Didžioji 26; ☏ 279 1644 [4 F5]
Open 10.00–17.00 except Sun–Mon (by appointment only). Free admission.
It would almost be easier to describe what this eclectic art museum does not contain, rather than what it does. From his arrival in the USA in 1949, Kazys combined his work in op art with a passion for collecting just at the time when prices were low and quantities high. He had as much an eye for Chinese painting as he did for British first editions, Italian Renaissance furniture or Lithuanian cartography. Throughout the museum the best of old Europe combines with the best of modern America and the map collection has no equal anywhere. There are 170 maps in total, nearly all of them of Lithuania and the surrounding region. Ample space and light are provided for the fascinating collection of modern art. Although born in 1917, Kazys was still painting in the studio at the top of this house in 2005. The studio can usually be visited, as can the Gothic brick cellars, which date from the 15th century. The museum is open only by appointment so it is essential to email (kvmuziejus@lnm.lt) or phone ahead, or make arrangements through a travel agent who works with Lithuania.

Vilnius Picture Gallery Didžioji 4; ☏ 212 4258 [2 G4]
Open 12.00–18.00, Sun 12.00–17.00, closed Mon. Admission 5Lt.
This state-run gallery shows in chronological order the development of painting in Lithuania and there are some real gems to discover, in particular where the main art

movements of 19th-century Europe are reflected in Lithuanian art. The gallery's first rooms begin with portraits, some dating as far back as the 16th century. The portraits of former rulers give an insight into the colourful history of the Polish-Lithuanian state.

Artists to look out for include Jan Rustemas, who became head of the city's first department of painting at Vilnius University in 1819. Born in Turkey to Greek parents, he lived in Warsaw and Berlin before bringing influences from these cities to Lithuania. He is credited with steering students away from classicism and towards Romanticism. Vincentas Dmachauskas's intense *Forest Fire* is a dramatic record of the destruction of the country's forests in the 19th century, monstrous fires that were also described by local writers and poets. There are also some evocative impressionist landscapes, such as Juozas Balzukevičius's *Across a Ryefield*.

CHURCHES

Vilnius Cathedral Katedros 1; ☎ 261 1127 [2 F2]
Open 09.00–20.00.

There is more to this grandiose display of neo-classicism than meets the eye. The Chapel of St Casimir inside is a flamboyant Baroque masterpiece with some breathtaking stucco work, while the cathedral's creepy crypt reaches into the bowels of the earth to reveal a fascinating cross-section of history, from the pagan to the present.

The cathedral occupies the site of what was once an ancient, open pagan temple revered by Lithuanians and dedicated to the worship of Perkūnas, god of thunder and fire. According to some accounts, toads, grass-snakes and other sacred creatures were kept nearby, ready for sacrifice on an altar that stood about 5m high. A fire blazed in a hollow in the temple, kept alight day and night. Virgins chosen for their beauty had the task of keeping the temple flames burning. If they failed, they were drowned with a cat and a snake, or were buried alive.

Vilnius Cathedral, belltower

Over the 800 years since these pagan times, five consecutive cathedral buildings have been built on the site, each in turn ravaged by fire, flood or war. Twelve different floors can be identified in the crypt, right down to the pagan altar itself. The earliest floor, dating from the 13th century, is now 3m deep. One or two glazed terracotta tiles that have survived from this time are on show by the entrance. You can also make out the top of the doorway of the very first cathedral, built by Mindaugas, the man who unified the Baltic tribes for the first time. He was baptised with his family around 1251, and erected a cathedral, a square building with a massive tower, shortly afterwards. The pagan lords and tribes were not happy with this sudden conversion, and when they killed Mindaugas ten years later, the building was converted for use as a temple.

Grand Duke Jogaila converted to Christianity in 1387, uniting Lithuania and Poland. He took the name Wladislaw (Ladislaus) and built a church here dedicated to St Ladislaus and Poland's patron saint Stanislaus. This stood until a fire in 1419. Grand

Churches

Duke Vytautas rebuilt it as a huge, Gothic, red-brick cathedral full of expressive architectural detail. It stood almost 8m taller than the present cathedral, and was completed only in 1430, the year Vytautas died. It was damaged by fire on several occasions in the coming 300 years, and was repeatedly rebuilt and restored. But this was marshy ground, and in the mid-1700s the foundations started sinking. Cracks appeared and in 1769 a severe storm blew down the south tower, killing six people.

Extensive reconstruction giving the cathedral its final shape started in 1783, according to a design by Laurynas Stuoka-Gucevičius. His idea, fashionable at the time, was to give the appearance, inside and out, of a real Greek temple. In fact, the neo-classical style is very rare for a cathedral. Stuoka-Gucevičius also designed Vilnius Town Hall, the palace at Verkiai, and also the wonderful circular church in the village of Sudervė, 25km northwest of Vilnius. The cathedral was his last great work.

The great crypt was the final resting place for grand dukes, archbishops, noblemen and their families. There are about 20 vaults under the floor of the naves and chapels. Some have yet to be discovered, undisturbed behind thick walls. The remains of Alexander, Grand Duke of Lithuania and King of Poland at the turn of the 16th century, and the wives of Sigismund Augustus – Elzbieta and Barbora Radvilaitė – were discovered in 1931. They were moved through the crypt to a hauntingly lit mausoleum. Barbora has a special place in the nation's heart. She and Sigismund were married out of love and kept their union a secret from the scheming nobles of the Polish-Lithuanian Commonwealth until she died mysteriously in 1551.

Under the Soviets, Vilnius Cathedral was used as a car repair garage. The three huge statues of saints Helena, Casimir and Stanislaus on the pediment were hauled down and demolished. After Stalin's death in 1953, the building became an art gallery. Finally, during the first congress of national revival in 1988, it was declared that the cathedral would be returned to the Church. Eight years later, after independence, replicas of the saints' statues were returned to their place on the grand façade.

The curious cupola that conflicts with the cathedral's overall design stands out as the stunning Baroque Chapel of St Casimir, a survivor of the earlier cathedral building. With red marble from Galicia, black and brown marble from the Carpathian Mountains, lavish stucco, and 17th-century frescoes, the chapel is a feast for the eyes. Exquisitely decorated by Italian masters over a period of 14 years from 1622, for the sum of 500,000 gold coins, it was built as a final resting place for the remains of St Casimir, the patron saint of Lithuania, who died in 1484.

Casimir was the youngest son of a wealthy family whose brothers and sisters became kings and queens of European states through lineage and marriage. The pious Casimir, however, was more interested in charity and would go to the cathedral to pray even at night. When he died from tuberculosis at the age of 25, it was rumoured that his coffin could cure illness and disease. A fresco on one side of the chapel shows the legend of Uršulė, a sick orphan who prayed beneath the coffin and found herself miraculously cured. The fresco on the wall opposite shows the moment when the coffin was opened by clergy to see if the body was still well preserved – the sign of a saint. It was, of course, and Casimir was canonised in 1602.

Churches

The chapel has some odd features. A 17th-century retable (a decorative panel at the back of an altar) shows a Madonna and Child. The Madonna has a surprisingly broad smile, very unusual for this kind of reverent artwork. In front of it, a silver-coated portrait shows St Casimir with three hands. Some say this was to emphasise his generosity – he gave as if from three hands. Look up into the cupola and you'll see beasts and objects finely moulded from stucco – an elephant for moderation (an elephant never eats more than his/her share), an elk to prevent rash decisions, and a mirror to see both sides of an argument.

The chapel nearest the entrance on the southern side is now known as the 'Deportees Chapel' because of the recent memorials that have been erected there to the many senior figures in the church who were persecuted in Soviet times. One of the statues is of Mečislovas Reinys, who was Archbishop of Vilnius before his arrest in 1947. He died in 1953 in Vladimir Prison near Moscow. Another is of Vincentas Borisevičius, Bishop of Telšiai until he was executed in 1947 for the 'crime' of being a 'bourgeois leader'. His final words were: 'Your hour of victory is brief; the future is mine; Christ will be victorious, just as Lithuania will be victorious.' It would be 40 years before he was proved right.

Church of St Anne Maironio 8; ☎ 261 4805 [2 H3]
Open 08.30–18.00.
A masterpiece of late Gothic, the enchanting façade features 33 shapes and sizes of red bricks arranged in flamboyant patterns. Its intricate towers, spires and

narrow windows were enough to enchant Napoleon, who in an oft-quoted remark said that he wished he could carry it back to Paris on the palm of his hand. He is, in fact, unlikely to have said such a thing, since like the rest of Europe in 1812 he disliked Gothic intensely as an outmoded style. Lithuanians saw Napoleon as a liberator from the grip of Tsarist Russia and probably concocted this story themselves. The French leader stationed some of his cavalry in St Anne's and most of its stained glass was broken and the wax ceilings destroyed by the soldiers' campfires.

The mystery of who designed the church endures to this day. One tale tells of a talented young Lithuanian apprentice named Jonas who helped his master from Belarus in the initial stages of construction before going to study architecture abroad. On his return he mocked his old master's work and completed the church in a flourish while the offended master vanished for several years. During this time Jonas married the master's daughter and settled into the family home. Late one stormy night, the master returned and insisted on Jonas showing him the brickwork. On the scaffolding, the more Jonas enthusiastically explained his work, the more envy the master felt. Eventually he pushed Jonas over the edge. Jonas caught hold of a piece of overhanging wood, but the master took a brick and brought it crashing down on Jonas's head. This tale of the outré may be mere legend, but it is strange how the lower part of the façade appears so much more austere than the rest. It is also true that in written records there were two architects, one known simply as 'Johannes', the other not mentioned at all.

Bernadine Church Maironio 10; ☏ 260 9292 [2 H3]
Open 08.30-18.00.

More than just the Gothic backdrop to St Anne's, the Bernadine Church is impressive in its sheer size. The vaulting is wondrous, but tragically the rest of the interior did not escape the ravages of the centuries. Fire, war and neglect left it to rot until 1994 when it was returned to the brethren of St Francis. Students from Vilnius Art Academy have slowly been renovating it ever since. Mass in English is held here every Sunday at 17.00.

Church of St Casimir Didžioji 34; ☏ 212 1715 [4 G5]
Open 10.00–18.00.

The oldest Baroque church in Vilnius, St Casimir's was founded by Jesuits in 1604. Named after Lithuania's patron saint, who had just been canonised, it's modelled on Il Gesu in Rome, the Jesuits' much-imitated mother church, but with characteristically Lithuanian twin spires set on top. St Casimir's has suffered many abuses through the centuries, including 20 years of humiliation as the Soviets' museum of atheism. Locals especially recall the prime exhibit – a re-creation of Inquisition torture implements, displayed to show the cruelty of the medieval Catholic Church. Now it is back in the safe hands of the original owners. The glittering crown on the central dome symbolises the royal family that Casimir came from (see *Vilnius Cathedral*, page 143). It was placed there in 1942.

Church of St Catherine Vilniaus 30 [I D4]
Closed to the public.
This rather intimidating structure originally belonged to a Benedictine convent founded in 1618. Following a series of fires, it was rebuilt between 1741 and 1753 by the Vilnius-born Polish architect Jan Krzyzstof Glaubitz, who also designed the extraordinary Basilian Gates. In order to overcome the restricted nature of the site, he adopted an audacious design based on a nave which is as high as it is long. The exterior features an elaborate rear-facing gable as a counterbalance to the majestic twin-towered façade. The interior is richly furnished, but has not been accessible for many years because of ongoing restoration work.

Church of the Holy Spirit Dominikonų 8; ℡ 262 9595 [I E4]
Open 07.00–18.00.
A Dominican friary established in Vilnius in 1501 gave Dominikonų Street its name. Its extravagant Church of the Holy Spirit, a lavish display of Baroque furnishings and decoration that are almost Rococo in appearance, is a suitable setting for several hauntings and unexplained events. The interior was ravaged by fire in the 18th century and almost completely remade. Its huge crypt, which extends underground even beyond the walls of the church, was used to bury corpses from the Napoleonic wars and, before that, plague victims. The bodies remain incredibly well preserved, stacked up on top of each other. It is not possible to go down there.

Churches

Strangely, the church was not closed by the Soviets and remained a place of worship throughout the last century. Today it is the religious heart of Vilnius's Polish community. The eye of the visitor is drawn immediately to the altarpiece, which depicts a vision of Christ as he appeared in a miracle to a local nun in 1931. The painting, *Divine Mercy*, was completed by the Vilnius artist Eugenijus Kazimierovskis (1873–1939) in 1934 but only after ten attempts to portray the vision as accurately as possible. The inscription, 'Jezu ufam tobie' means 'Jesus, I trust in thee'. To the Polish community, the wide rays of red and white light represent their flag. The painting was hidden in the countryside through most of the Soviet period, only being brought back to this church in 1986 at the beginning of the perestroika period. Its long-term location is a matter of considerable dispute, as a chapel over the road has been built to house it but the Polish community is eager to keep it where it now stands and where Pope Paul II saw it on his 1993 visit to Vilnius.

Statues of King David and angel musicians adorn the beautifully carved case that protects an organ made in 1776 by Adam Casparini. This is the oldest organ in Vilnius and a model of it is being built for Christ Church at the University of Rochester, New York. It should be finished in 2008.

Church of the Holy Spirit (Orthodox) Aušros Vartų 10; ✆ 212 7765 [4 G6]
Open 08.00–18.00.
The most revered of the city's Russian Orthodox churches stands in a peaceful courtyard away from the bustle of Aušros Vartų Street. There is not actually a

great deal to distinguish it from the surrounding Catholic churches, it having been rebuilt by the genius of the late Baroque period Jan Krzysztof Glaubitz after a fire in 1749. But the most important feature makes it a popular place of pilgrimage for Orthodox Christians – the well-preserved bodies of saints Anthony, Ivan and Eustace, killed by pagans in 1347 for not renouncing their faith. The three lie in a glass-topped case shrouded in red most of the year, in white during Christmas and black during Lent. Should you be in Vilnius on 26 June, however, visit this church to feel the healing spirit that is said to envelop it when the bodies are unveiled.

Church of St John Šv Jono 12; ☏ 261 1795 [2 F3]
Open for services Sun 11.00–13.00.
Immediately after Grand Duke Jogaila shed his pagan beliefs to convert to Christianity in 1387, he commissioned this church, completed 40 years later. Originally Gothic, the awe-inspiring Baroque façade you see today was designed, once again by Jan Krzysztof Glaubitz, in the 1740s. The interior, accessible from a university courtyard, boasts a high altar consisting of no fewer than ten interconnected altars. One of the many memorials inside is dedicated to the memory of Adam Mickiewicz.

Church of SS Peter and Paul Antakalnio 1; ☏ 234 0229 [*Vilnius* map]
Open 07.00–19.00.
One of Vilnius's most stunning Baroque churches, with twin-tower façade and a

Churches

central dome, the magnificent Church of SS Peter and Paul was completed in 1685. It was built on the site of a wooden church that had been burned by pillaging Russians during their destructive invasion 30 years earlier. This was a time of almost constant war, but churches like this continued to rise up. The man who commissioned the Church of SS Peter and Paul was Mykolaj Casimir Pac, Field Hetman of the Grand Duchy of Lithuania. His appeal to the Mother of God above the church entrance is not for strength in war, but for an end to war: 'Regina pacis fundanos in pace' (Queen of peace, protect us in peace), although this could simply have been a playful pun on the patron's name.

Mythological scenes and strange creatures, flowers, trees, and over 2,000 human figures in stucco decorate the rich interior. Baroque also placed a lot of emphasis on death, which accounts for the array of skulls, skeletons, dragons and demons immediately on the left and right as you walk in. Criminals were not allowed to enter any further into the nave than this point and the ugly images were meant to remind them of the consequences of sin.

In the amazing figures and images in stucco, stories can be made out. Many relate to the sea, since Peter and Paul were both fishermen, and possibly the main curiosity in the entire church is an enormous, boat-shaped chandelier, hanging from the cupola like a grand cluster of jewels, magnificently catching the light.

If the bottom of the kettledrum close to the altar to Mary on the left appears blackened, this is because it also doubled in times of war as a cooking pot and a bath for the soldiers.

Gates of Dawn Aušros Vartų 12; ☎ 212 3513 [4 G7]
Open 09.00–17.00.
One of the essential sights on any trip to Vilnius, the 16th-century Gates of Dawn – originally part of the city's fortifications – now hold a small chapel housing a gold-and-silver holy image of the Virgin Mary, the Madonna of Mercy, which overlooks the street through open windows. Locals cross themselves every time they walk underneath it, while the most devout of worshippers crawl piously on their knees up steps from a doorway on the left. Unless you want to crawl too, climb past them to inspect the miracle-working icon up close. Afterwards, pass out of the gates to find part of the original city wall stretching down a dark back alley towards the Artillery Bastion.

LANDMARKS
Europa Tower Konstitucijos 7a; ☎ 248 7171
Open at weekends. Free admission.
Thirty-three floors up in the Europa Tower, the tallest skyscraper in the Baltic states, completed in 2004, the view of central Vilnius is unrivalled. It's perfect for a bird's-eye perspective on where the best vacant lots of real estate are hiding. And getting to the top is free. There is only one restriction: the Europa Tower is a caffeine-fuelled office building, which means that the resident companies do not want unruly groups of sightseers milling around, clogging up the lifts. So access to the public is only at the weekend. Otherwise, groups can call ahead to book visits on weekdays.

After an ear-popping elevator ride to the top, the open air is invigorating. The 33rd floor is an open terrace facing southwards, while the vista to the north is from office space that can be rented out for seminars or private parties, for which food and drink can be ordered from one of the eateries in the Europa shopping centre below. Both views stretch the full 180 degrees.

It's the panorama to the south that grabs the attention, taking in the Old Town, the river and the brand new smattering of nearby skyscrapers. From this height, however, some of the buildings become virtually indistinguishable and the tall glass barrier also slightly obscures the visibility. But it's the thrill of standing on one of the highest viewpoints for hundreds of kilometres around that you should come for.

Looking north, you can see Vilnius's ragbag of old and new suburbs – the tumbledown wooden shacks of Šnipiškės, which will soon disappear to make way for new buildings, and in the distance masses of identical Soviet-era residential blocks.

Gariūnai Market

For years one of the biggest open-air markets in eastern Europe, these days Gariūnai is dominated by poor-quality products from China and Turkey. The sprawling market stands in the shadow of the city's water-heating plant, about 10km west of the city centre on the road to Kaunas. The stalls sell pushchairs, lightbulbs, pirate DVDs, hi-fis, bad coffee, you name it. Some of the clothes sellers have recently gone upmarket with permanent stalls that actually resemble small shops. The rest, though, is set up from scratch early in the morning, which explains why so many of the salespeople yawn at you. In the early 1990s it was rumoured you could buy weapons here by finding the man with the toy gun on his bonnet. The best times to go are weekend mornings; by noon the market is closing up. Watch your wallet/handbag.

Paneriai Agrastų 17; ↘ 260 2001
Out in the forests to the southwest of Vilnius lies the village of Paneriai, consisting mostly of close-knit wooden houses, unpaved streets, a railway track and stray dogs. Close by, about 100,000 people were murdered in a clearing, their bodies burned in pits. Most of them were Jews from Vilnius – a fact ignored in the wording on the memorials here until 1990. In fact, a dance hall was raised on the site in the early Soviet period. Today, the pits are displayed, the whole place eerily quiet except for the occasional passing train. It is notoriously hard to find due to the shameful lack of signposting. Take a train going to Trakai and get off at the Paneriai stop. Walk along the lane that runs more-or-less parallel to the tracks in the same direction the train is heading. The memorial lies at the end of the road, after about a kilometre. A small branch of the Lithuanian State Jewish Museum displays some photographs, but it has no set opening times and is closed in winter.

Television Tower Sausio 13-osios 10; ↘ 252 5333 [*Vilnius* map]
Open 12.00–21.00; admission 15Lt (children 6Lt).

Landmarks

Venture out into the 'sleeping districts' of Vilnius's high-rise suburbs at least once during your stay and experience this Soviet vision of the 1970s space age, with an unequalled panorama from its 55th-floor restaurant. Christened Paukščių Takas, Lithuanian for 'Milky Way', when it opened in 1980, the restaurant is 165m up and rotates slowly so that a full circle is completed in 50 minutes. On a clear day you can see up to 70km in every direction (don't come if the sky is thick with cloud), when you will discover just how amazingly green Lithuania really is. Coniferous forests stretch out to the horizon. The Old Town and Vilnius's landmark buildings are clearly visible just to the east. Beyond, you can spy on Belarus, the last dictatorship in Europe, only 40km away.

Before you shoot up in the high-speed elevator, you have a choice at the reception of either paying the entry fee and then having the freedom of the menu, or taking one of four set meals for about double the price, which includes the entry fee. We recommend the former, since the set meals are more a convenient tool for the restaurant when coping with groups.

The wording on the menu is worth the price of admission alone. 'Meat collection' consists of 'fried pork, fried neck with dried plumps'. The wonderfully titled 'Mischief of frost' is 'fruit and berry ice cream, berries and fruit'.

Before you leave, pay your respects to the 14 Lithuanian civilians who died here defending the Television Tower from Soviet tanks on the night of 13 January 1991. A small exhibition remembering this tragic event can be found on the ground floor. Outside, granite markers show the precise places where the victims were crushed beneath tanks or shot. Sadly, the surroundings look a little unkempt, weeds protruding through the concrete blocks.

However, the tower comes to life in December when it becomes what is claimed to be the tallest artificial Christmas tree in the world, with fairy lights stretching up its entire height.

Verkiai Palace Žaliujų ežerų 47; ☎ 271 1618
Open 09.00–17.00 except Sat–Sun. Admission 3Lt.

The remains of a superb classical mansion stand on a hill just to the north of Vilnius. The land here belonged to grand dukes until 1387, when Jogaila, on his conversion to Christianity, granted it to the new diocese of Vilnius to be used by the bishops as a summer residence. In 1780, a huge palace was constructed here, but Napoleon's soldiers ravaged it in 1812. Soon after that the central part of the palace was pulled down.

Today, the rooms in the remaining wings of the palace contain a great deal of handsome, intricate woodwork and some attractive painted ceilings. There's also a lovely view of the forested River Neris valley below, and at the very end of the ridge is a fireplace surrounded by stones. A legend tells how a sacred fire was once tended on this spot by a pagan priest and beautiful virgins.

Walk down the long flight of steps to an old mill, recently renovated into a restaurant, named Verkių Vandens Malūnas. It serves delicious homemade meals and has peaceful outdoor seating overlooking the river in summer.

Landmarks

Vilnius University Universiteto 3; ☏ 261 1795 [2 F3]
Open 09.00–17.00 except Sun.

The oldest university in eastern Europe is a maze of 12 courtyards, corridors, halls and towers. It is a delight to explore and usually no one will mind if you do. An absurd practice of selling tickets at the gate was recently established, but we recommend you walk directly through with a sense of purpose, pretending you're a visiting professor or a mature student. A basic map of the complicated layout is at Universiteto 7.

Founded by the Jesuits in 1570 and given university status in 1579, Vilnius University has not always been allowed to flourish and contribute to the cultural, social and political life of the city. Many of its students and professors have aided the resistance against virtually every occupation, often to find themselves persecuted, even executed. The entire university was closed by the Russian Tsarist authorities in 1832 for backing the failed rebellion the year before. It stayed closed until 1919, the year after Lithuanian independence was regained.

At the far end of the initial Sarbievijus Courtyard is the lovely Littera bookshop, whose walls and ceiling were painstakingly decorated by local painter Antanas Kmieliauskas in preparation for the university's 400th birthday in 1979. In fact, the university as a whole is in good condition because of the extensive renovations made in time for that event. Another artist, Petras Repšys, created the stunning fresco cycle in the Centre for Lithuanian Studies next door, working at it for nine years, finishing in 1985.

Up a flight of steps from the Sarbievijus Courtyard is the Great Courtyard, dominated on one side by the monumental Baroque façade of St John's Church. There is an almost Mediterranean flavour to the open arcades around the courtyard, while faded frescoes from the 18th century show figures who influenced the early part of the life of the university. An arch in the western side of the courtyard leads to a small but charmingly leafy courtyard beside the Observatory, the walls of which are decorated with the signs of the Zodiac.

CEMETERIES

Vilnius has a number of cemeteries set amid the hills around the city centre that are really worth visiting, if time permits, for they reflect aspects of the city's tumultuous history. Reach Antakalnis Cemetery by walking beyond the Church of SS Peter and Paul up busy Antakalnio Street, bearing right onto L Sapiegos then turning right onto progressively quieter Kuosų and Karių. The Bernadine Cemetery is found, eerie and cut off from the rest of the city, in Užupis, at the end of a little lane off Polocko Street. Rasa Cemetery is best reached by strolling up Rasų Street away from Subačiaus in the Old Town.

Antakalnis Cemetery (Antakalnio kapinės) [*Vilnius* map]
A calm and peaceful place that brings together much of Vilnius's modern history, the biggest public cemetery in Vilnius has elegantly carved old memorial stones covering the rolling, tree-shaded landscape, the crosses and tombs adorned and inscribed in Lithuanian, Russian and Polish. Following the paved path into the

cemetery, you find a series of identical stone crosses over to the left dedicated to Polish soldiers killed during World War I – as bloody and tragic a conflict in eastern Europe as it was in the West. By taking paths to the right, you'll find broadly chiselled Soviet-era statues in the Socialist Realist style, commemorating those poets and political leaders who toed the party line. Cut into a hill at the cemetery's heart is a sweeping, semi-circular memorial to the 14 people who died defending the Television Tower and the Parliament building in January 1991.

Bernadine Cemetery (Bernadinų kapinės)
Beautifully perched on a high bank above the little River Vilnia at the far end of the quaint suburb of Užupis, is this tranquil spot, tightly packed with lopsided metal crosses and tiny, uneven plots. Founded in 1810, this quiet retreat holds the last resting places of university academics and painters. Over the long years, trees have gently elbowed their way between the tombs, making them even more irregular, gradually spilling through railings that fence off the graves. Desolate and wonderfully gloomy, you will find no calmer place in Vilnius.

Rasa Cemetery (Rasų kapinės)
Deceptively isolated, this hill of crosses contains the graves of famous Lithuanians like Jonas Basanavičius, the founder at the end of the 19th century of the first Lithuanian-language newspaper *Aušra* (Dawn). He lies close to the chapel, while uphill from the main entrance lies the tombstone of revered painter and composer M K Čiurlionis. Right next to the entrance, however, is a more controversial site –

the family plot of the Polish leader Josef Pilsudski, the man responsible for Poland's annexation of Vilnius in 1920. He was buried in Krakow, but his heart was cut out and buried here, in this tomb. Rasa Cemetery has been a place of spiritual reverence also during troubled times. More daring Lithuanians gathered here in October 1956 to protest the suppression of the Hungarian uprising.

Vilnius Cathedral

11 Beyond the city

Vilnius offers a wide choice of places to visit for a half- or full-day excursion and it is well worth extending a short break to allow time for these. Kaunas definitely requires a full day and staying the night is also worthwhile to give more time to cover what it offers. A half-day in Trakai is enough for seeing the spectacular Island Castle, but not for walking around the lake and the charming village. Europa Park can be covered in half a day; about two hours is probably sufficient to cover the array of sculptures, but in good weather a leisurely day could happily be spent there.

EUROPA PARK

Off the road that passes Verkai and the Green Lakes (follow the signs), 10km north of Vilnius; ℘ 237 7077; www.europosparkas.lt
Open 09.00–sunset. Admission 20Lt.

There's a lot of talk about the concept of Europe in Lithuania, just as there is in the other EU countries. Here, however, it is brought to life just a few kilometres from the 'centre of Europe' as defined in 1989 by the French National Geographic Institute. Although only about 10km north of Vilnius, access by public transport is very difficult, so it is worth joining a group tour or sharing a taxi with others. Europa Park is an open-air museum of mostly bizarre modern sculptures in a woodland and meadow setting (take insect repellent in July), with exhibits specially created for the site by around 100 different artists from 30 countries around the world.

Founded in 1991, it is the brainchild of the Lithuanian sculptor Gintaras Karosas who had conceived the idea a few years earlier while still a teenager and who did much of the preparatory work of clearing the site with his own hands. He created the pivotal *Monument of the Centre of Europe* which features a pyramid and indications of the direction and distances to a range of worldwide capitals, of which the furthest away is Wellington in New Zealand. Karosas was also responsible for the heavily symbolic *Infotree* by the park entrance, which has gained an entry in the *Guinness Book of Records* for being the world's largest artwork of television sets. There are 3,000 in all, arranged (when viewed from above) in the shape of a tree, with a decaying statue of Lenin in the middle.

Chair Pool by the American Dennis Oppenheim is the most popular work, and also the most humorous, as its subject is exactly what the title suggests, a giant chair with a small pool instead of a seat. The success of this led to the commissioning of a second composition from Oppenheim, *Drinking Structure with Exposed Kidney Pool*, consisting of a hut dipping down towards the water. Other sculptures guaranteed to catch the eye are Magdalena Abakanowicz's *Space of Unknown Growth*, a group of 22 concrete boulders; Jon Barlow Hudson's *Cloud Hands*, which consists of four granite blocks seemingly suspended in the air; and the 6m-high *Woman Looking at the Moon* by the Mexican Javier Cruz.

KAUNAS

That Kaunas was a capital for 20 years, from 1920 to 1940, becomes quickly apparent when walking through the town from the bus or railway station into the town. Like Bonn for Germany in the post-War era, Kaunas was officially a 'provisional" capital, as the Lithuanian government was forced to flee there when the Poles were clearly not willing to give up Vilnius. If the former presidential palace now seems modest, this did not prevent the government from building ministries, museums and churches that over 60 years later have not lost any of their grandeur even if they have now lost their original function. Other legacies from that era are two funicular railways and two large river bridges.

The most famous resident of Kaunas known worldwide was **Dr Ludoviko Zamenhof** who invented Esperanto whilst still running his medical practice. A street is named after him, and a travel agency, Bonvoje, based there offers tours with Esperanto-speaking guides. Two names which even day visitors will remember are **Darius** and **Girėnas**, two pilots who in 1933 almost succeeded in flying non-stop from New York to Kaunas but sadly crashed and were killed in East Prussia. A sports stadium and an airport are named after them, as is a major street. The wreck of their plane, together with their blood-stained shirts, are displayed in the War Museum. Their statues are amongst the largest in Kaunas and their portraits are on the ten litas banknote.

Being a crossing on the **Nemunas (Memel)** River, and the junction where the **Neris** River joins it, Kaunas has for centuries been a frequent battle ground

KAUNAS

0   400m
0   400yds

© Bradt Travel Guides Ltd

N

Bradt

Neris

VILJAMPOLĖS TILTAS

JONAVOS

ŽEMAIČIŲ

Babilonas

ŽALIAKALNIO

The Resurrection

MACKEVIČIAUS

SAVANORIŲ

Devils Museum

Pompėja

Žaliakalnis
Funicular

PUTVINSKIO

Čiurlionis
Art Museum

Military Museum

Freedom Monument

Synagogue

Central
post
office

DONELAIČIO

VIENYBĖS
AIKŠTĖ

Neris

Castle

ŠV GERTRUDOS

St George

Holy
Trinity

Yakata

Presidential
palace

Vytautas
the Great

St Michael the Archangel
& Museum for the Blind

Medical Museum

Cathedral

Zoological
Museum

Kaunas

LAISVĖS ALĖJA

tal Museum

Town hall

ROTUŠĖS
AIKŠTĖ

Kavinė

Internetas

VILNIAUS

City Garden

MAIRONIO

Viva

Mykolas
Žilinskas
Art Gallery

DAUKANTO

GEDIMINO

erature
eramics
useum

Jonas
aciulis
cronis

Perkūnas
House

Minotel

St Francis Xavier

Lithuanian Folk
Instruments Museum

Best Western
Santaka

KĘSTUČIO

Arenapizza

Vytautas

ALEKSOTO
TILTAS

Tado Blindos Smuklė

KARALIAUS MINDAUGO

MARVELĖ

Nemunas

Aleksotas
Funicular

MINKOVSKIŲ

between all Lithuania's largest neighbours eager to subject it. Napoleon fought for it in 1812 and the Russians then built a circle of fortresses to defend what was the westernmost outpost of their empire. The capture of these forts by the Germans in 1915 would lead to their victory over Tsarist Russia and then to Lithuanian independence. Throughout the 19th century the Russians banned building on the nearby hills and allowed none in the town to have more than two storeys, so concerned were they at the potential threat from the Germans. They took no interest in preserving the town's varied architectural legacy or in contributing to a new one.

When the German government was reluctantly forced to make Bonn a provisional capital in 1949, they at least had a serious cultural centre on which to base it. Kaunas by 1920 had declined to little more than a dilapidated village. One journalist described it as 'a cramped and exceedingly unhealthy town of mean streets and wretched wooden houses'. Another wrote of the open drains beside all the main roads and the tram-cars dragged along by a single horse. All visitors complained of the lack of hygiene in the one small hotel in the town but only one diplomat admitted to solving this problem by finding 'une petite amie' who offered much more congenial accommodation.

It would be the 1930s before the government unofficially planned on the basis that Kaunas would be a permanent capital. Most of the majestic buildings along and beside **Laisvės Alėja** reflect this change in policy. Vytautas Landsbergis, whose son with the same name would lead Lithuania to independence around 1990, was one of several architects involved in building a serious Kaunas at that time. By 1940, this development would become so extensive and so solid that it would survive 50 years of Soviet rule.

Kaunas was often at the forefront of Lithuanian resistance to Russia, whatever the nature of the St Petersburg or Moscow regime. Two uprisings took place in the 19th century, in 1831 and 1863; then in 1972 a 19-year-old student **Romas Kalanta** burning himself to death in public became the precursor of many other demonstrations against Moscow.

Since independence Kaunas has not really found a new role for itself as Vilnius is eager to make up for the 20 years it did not have as a capital. New political movements no longer start here and most of the 19 mayors the town had between 1991 and 2005 showed little sense of direction, a state of affairs Vilnius was happy to exploit. With Vilnius as European capital of culture in 2009, Kaunas has an even tougher task in presenting itself to the outside world as an independent entity. However a trebling of property prices between 2003 and 2006 shows that business is now keen to bring it to life again.

Getting there and away

No-frills flights with Ryanair from London Stansted direct to Kaunas started in autumn 2005 as did Wizzair flights from Warsaw and were followed early in 2006 by services from Dublin and Stockholm. So tourism could perhaps help it to revive. Whilst discussions for such flights had been going on intermittently for several

Kaunas

years previously, it seemed that only in 2005 was Kaunas's Karmelava Airport willing to accept the terms no-frills carriers dictate. This should lead to an enormous expansion of tourism and to Kaunas being seen as a destination in its own right, rather than just as a petrol station or toilet stop between Vilnius and the coast. Up-to-date information can be found on the Tourist Board website (*http://visit.kaunas.lt*) or on the airport website (*www.kaunasair.lt*). The airport is 12km north of the city and minibus 120 runs regularly along the main road beside the airport but does not come into it. The fare is 1.50Lt.

Bus 29 comes into the airport and runs to the main bus station but visitors will probably want to alight one or two stops before then, near to the sights and to most hotels. Buy tickets for 0.90Lt. Taxis are best avoided as they are not properly metered in Kaunas. With the help of a local person it should be possible to get a taxi into the town for 20–25Lt. Foreigners are usually charged at least double this. However, given the range of public transport options, there is never any need to use a taxi.

The bus or train journey to Kaunas from Vilnius takes about 75 minutes and costs around £2/$4 one-way. There are eight trains a day but buses and minibuses leave at least every half-hour from around 05.30 until 23.30.

Getting around

The bus and train station are about 200m apart, and several bus and trolleybus routes serve both of them. It is possible to walk towards the Castle taking most of the main sights en route, and then to take a trolleybus back or to do the reverse, which is how the tour below is based. Visitors continuing to the coast should take the hydrofoil to Nida along the Nemusas River and then across the Curonian Lagoon. The trolleybuses to note are numbers 1, 5, 7 and 13 which head for the Castle in a westerly direction along Kęstučio, Kanto, Nemuno and Gimnazijos. They return along Ožeškienės and Donelaičio as most of the streets in central Kaunas are one-way, either eastbound or westbound. In late 2005 tickets bought from the driver cost 0.75Lt and those bought in kiosks cost 0.60Lt.

Accommodation

Visitors who decide to stay overnight now have a good choice of hotels from which to choose.

Kaunas Laisvės 79; ☏ 37 750850; f 37 750851; e kanuas@kaunashotel.lt; www.kaunashotel.lt

Having first opened in 1999, the Kaunas is the most conveniently located hotel. It is on Laisvės from which no museum, church or restaurant is more than 10 mins' walk. It is expanding all the time and by 2006 most rooms will have baths rather than just showers, and AC, together with tea and coffee making facilities. Many have a view over Laisvės and therefore over town life, but double-glazing ensures that the visual side of any outside activity reaches the rooms, but not the sound. The restaurant is built into a former brewery and the wall paintings enhance the country feel. However, the portrait over the stairs is surprisingly incongruous; it is of the 19th-century Bishop Valančius who struggled to keep

Kaunas

the Lithuanian language alive when it was under severe threat from the Soviet authorities but he is in fact best remembered as a high-profile temperance campaigner.

Minotel Kuzmos 8; ↘ 37 203759; f 37 220355; e minotel@kaunas.omnitel.net; www.minotel.lt
A smaller central hotel which is in fact the nearest one to Town Hall Square.

Best Western Santaka Gruodzio 21; ↘ 37 302702; fax 37 302700; e office@santanka.lt; www. santaka.lt
Not far from the Minotel, the Best Western has skilfully been integrated into a 19th-century brick building so rooms vary greatly in size and view. It is proud of its diverse clientele: the Dalai Lama has stayed here but so has the under-19 English football team.

Neris Donelaičio 27; ↘ 37 306100; f 306221; e info@takiojineris.com; www.takiojineris.com
Groups usually stay at the Neris which suffers from the fact that it dates from Soviet times. Whilst the exterior still makes this obvious, the interior was completed revamped in 1998 and further reconstruction has been undertaken since then.

Žaliakalnio (Green Hill) Savanorių 66; ↘ 37 321412; f 37 733769; e zaliakalnis@takiojineris.com; www. takiojineris.com
Tourists happy to start their day with a funicular ride into town can take advantage of the lower prices and extensive town views on offer here. Under the same management as the Neris.

Eating and drinking

For about the first ten years after the restoration of independence in 1990, it has to be admitted that Kaunas had a very poor choice of restaurants. This then suddenly changed and by 2005 about 30–40 could genuinely be recommended, many having websites as well. Doubtless this number will continue to increase. Many tourists never leave Laisvės Alėja for their meals, but a detour of just two to three hundred metres is well worthwhile.

Tado Blindos Smukle Kęstučio 93; ꜛ 202993
A good choice for local food, where beer rather than wine must be the staple drink and meat should take priority over fish.

Pompėja Putvinskio 38; ꜛ 422055; www.pompeja.lt
The quality of food offered has fortunately not suffered as a result of the number of groups who now eat here, nor should it be judged by the spelling and punctuation on the website. The serious visitor will probably prefer the quieter environment at lunchtime whilst others will want to enjoy the lively evenings that are provided through much of the summer. Italian is probably the most extensively represented cuisine in Kaunas.

Arenapizza Kęstučio 6; ꜛ 424242; www.arenapizza.lt
Concentrating on this one dish and with the size of the portions offered, few visitors will want to stray from this.

Yakata Valančiaus 14; ✆ 204512; www.yakata.lt
Japanese restaurants tend to be exclusive in Western Europe but in Kaunas has a wide
variety of fish dishes in an otherwise predominantly carnivore environment.

Viva Laisvės 53; ✆ 40004
On Laisvės itself, this is the best self-service restaurant and it spreads out of doors during
the summer.

What to see and do

Architecturally, central Kaunas is divided into two areas: in the **Old Town**
(**Senamiestis),** around the Castle and Town Hall Square, most buildings are from
the 19th century or earlier; the **New Town (Naujamiestis)** is centred on the
pedestrian precinct **Laisvės Alėja** which reflects a building frenzy in the 1930s
when it was privately assumed that Kaunas would become Lithuania's permanent
capital. However, the geometric layout of the New Town, with its long straight
avenues, dates from 1871.

Old Town

Kaunas Castle has clearly been the site of a fortification for at least a thousand
years but the precursor to the stone and brick building now in ruins probably dates
from the 13th century. Its 2m-thick walls and the deep moat suggest centuries of
bitter fighting but in fact none ever took place around Kaunas and the current

neglected state of the Castle results not from battles but from the Russians abandoning it in the 19th century and then from floods early in the 20th century. The **Church of St George**, is so close to the Castle and in similar brick that it seems part of the same complex but in fact is known to date from the early 15th century, when Christianity first came to Kaunas. It is currently (2005) closed for restoration and this is likely to last for several years. Between this church and the Town Hall Square is the **Seminary**, remarkable for the fact that it was allowed to function throughout the Soviet era and 500 priests graduated during that time. The attached **Holy Trinity Church** was used as a warehouse for much of that time, but was reconsecrated in 1982, eight years before the collapse of the Soviet Union. As a result, the interior was properly refurbished in time for the papal visit in 1993.

Town Hall Square (Rotušės Aikštė)

It is fortunate how little damage this square has suffered and much of it still looks as it would have done 200 years ago. Strict controls now prevent developers from changing any of the façades. Because of the Tsarist ban on buildings of more than two storeys, the **Town Hall** with its six-storey tower dating from the late 16th century still dominates the square much as it did when it was first built. It is hard to believe that the tower is only 53m high. Fortunately, each new ruler, including Soviet Russia, maintained it well and its obvious nickname of the 'White Swan' has again been passed down from regime to regime. Saturday is a good day to see the building in action, since most weddings still take place there. There is a **Ceramics**

Museum (*open Tue–Sun 11.00–17.00*) in the cellars; the entrance is precarious, down a narrow steep staircase with a ceiling not geared to anybody above average height. One cellar has a permanent exhibition of ceramics discovered in the city during archaeological excavations. Another is used for temporary exhibitions of works by local artists.

Fire, neglect and a constant change of ownership between various faiths, not to mention its use as a secondary school in the Soviet period, has left the **Church of St Francis** with a very bare interior. The exterior, built between 1666 and 1725 has kept its neo-Baroque façade and it is to be hoped that with the church now back in the hands of the Jesuits, a worthy interior can soon be built.

The statue which dominates the southwest corner of the square is of **Jonas Mačiulis Maironis** (1862–1932) Lithuania's most famous poet who was also Rector of the Seminary from 1909 until his death. The face may seem familiar as it is on the 20 litas banknote. Wedding couples leaving the Town Hall often have their photograph taken here. Maironis lived in the building behind the statue which is now the **Literature Museum** (*www.maironiomuziejus.lt; open Tue–Sat 09.00–17.00*). This covers not only his work but also that of many of his contemporaries. The collection was extended in 1999 to include literature produced from 1944 by the very large, and worldwide Lithuanian exile community. The museum website has extensive material in English about Lithuanian literature.

On the northwest side of the square are the 19th-century stables used by the postal service, which now house the **Museum of Posts and**

Telecommunications (*open Wed–Sun 10.00–18.00*). The stress here is in fact on the postal side and exhibits cover sorting, route maps, transport and staff uniforms. Telegrams, telex and fax transmission are also covered. There is an extensive display of stamps from the pre-War Republic and from the restoration of independence in 1991. Outside, a collection of horse-drawn carriages is being built up. Sadly, despite an extensive renovation in 2004, all the explanations are still only in Lithuanian.

The east side of the square used to consist of private houses, but these have been largely converted into shops and offices now with number 28 being the **Museum of the History of Lithuanian Medicine and Pharmacy** (*open Wed–Sun 11.00–18.00*), which has refitted a chemist's shop and dispensary as it would have looked in the 19th century. Some of the exhibits, however, go back to the 16th century and the shop could well have been functioning then. The origin of the equipment shows how international Kaunas had become during the 1800s. A pill-making machine is from Leipzig, an oil press from Luxembourg and a cash machine from the United States. A century before Viagra this pharmacy could offer its clients a herb called Erektosan. The museum also covers dentistry so has a drill operated by a foot pedal.

The **cathedral**, on the corner of Vilniaus and Town Hall Square, is the largest Gothic building in Lithuania although the interior is totally Baroque. The brickwork dates from the 15th century, with the woodwork and painting mainly from the 18th century. Its size is perhaps reflected in the fact that it has nine different altars. Being open in Soviet times, it was protected from the desecration that occurred then in so many other Kaunas churches. The poet Maironis is buried in the south wall.

Kaunas

Beyond Town Hall Square

Walking from Town Hall Square towards the Nemunas River along Aleksoto, another red-brick Gothic building stands out on the right hand side. This is **Perkūnas (Thunder) House.** Facts about its history and its use are distinctly lacking, but theories abound. Construction probably began in the 16th century and constant alterations were made until around 1800. The Hanseatic League may well have used it as their headquarters and in the 19th century a theatre operated here. The name comes from a figurine of the God of Thunder discovered in the 19th century. It is now a school but it is sometimes possible to see the interior.

Perilously close to the river is **Vytautas Church** named after the Lithuanian Duke who defeated the Teutonic Knights. Beside the road leading down to the river is a marker showing how far and how often flood waters have risen. However, the church has survived well from the 14th century, despite floods, looting by Napoleon's army and constant changes in ownership between orthodox and catholic communities. It is now in catholic hands.

Walking along the river for about 200m the third turning on the left is Zamenhofo and number 12, the **Lithuanian Folk Instruments Museum** (*open Wed–Sun 10.00–18.00*) is a collection of small houses set around a courtyard. The museum was founded in 1983 by the father of the current director who took it upon himself to collect as many traditional instruments as he could whilst they were still in good condition. They are all constructed from very simple pieces of wood or metal, but nonetheless produce very acceptable music. The staff seem equally adept at demonstrating wind, brass or string instruments and tours can be accompanied by tapes playing in the background. Returning to Vilniaus and continuing east using the underpass to cross Gimnazijos, on the left is the former **Presidential Palace** (open Tue–Sun 11.00–17.00) which opened in 2005 as a museum covering the 1920–40 period. It is remarkable how much worthwhile material has survived, given the speed of the Soviet take-over in 1940 and the danger for Lithuanians in keeping material from this 'bourgeois' regime. In its gardens are statues of the three presidents who lived there – Antanas Smetona, Aleksandras Stulginskis and Kazys Grinius. Stulginskis has the most confident pose, even though he is portrayed with a stick. Grinius is seated with a look of exhaustion. Smetona has the detached look of an undertaker, perhaps appropriate as he was the last President before the Soviet take-over in 1940. The palace is appropriately on the edge of the New Town, through which the walk now continues, and where this regime was to make such an architectural mark.

New Town

The New Town (Naujamiestis) is centred on the mile-long pedestrial precinct **Laisvės Alėja.** There have been attempts to ban smoking as well as cars here but these have not been successful. However, it is wide and windy enough for non-smokers not to be concerned over this. It runs from the former Presidential Palace in the west to the Church of St Michael in the east. Visitors should, however, be careful at the cross streets which cars are allowed to use.

Kaunas

LAISVĖS ALĖJA IN THE 1920s

In Kaunas there is no traffic problem, for one rarely sees a motor-car; the clatter of hoofs and drosky wheels over the cobbles takes the place of humming engines and the only other public conveyances are dilapidated and overcrowded trams, each pulled by a single horse.

There are plenty of interesting types to be found on this Unter den Linden of Kaunas: barefooted peasant women, their hair hidden under white or coloured cloths, carrying baskets filled with fruit; priests, hideously shaven-headed like many others of the male community, in long black cassocks and bowlers or panama; then there are the sallow-faced Jews, the bearded Russians and the pretty girls with characteristic Ltihuanian blue eyes and fair hair. Many look English and are well-dressed but sometimes they wear socks that leave an expanse of bare calf, a modern fashion that, who knows, may reach us yet.

At Laisvės 106, is the **Tadas Ivanauskas Zoological Museum** (*open Tue–Sun 11.00–19.00*), which claims to have 173,000 different items, although only 13,000 are on display. It is named after the founder, who managed to establish it in 1919, despite all the fighting going on around Kaunas at that time. A few labels are translated into English but most are still in just Russian and Lithuanian. Sadly little has been done here since the Soviet era, so whilst the building offers space, it does

The many Jews one passes are a strange contrast to the fair Lithuanians. The town has a large Jewish quarter, and half of the town's 120,000 population. Their restless energy has done much to help the trade revival of the Baltic states. The Kaunas market is the meeting-place of Jew and Gentile and although there is no love lost between the two, trade brings them together.

The Town Museum is only open for four hours on two days a week. I found it closed, but discovered the curator sitting on a bench outside. He received the suggestion that he should open the museum rather sourly until it transpired that I came from London, when his manner changed and he professed himself willing to show me anything I wished to see. The main exhibit is a picture of the Crucifixion, said to be an original Rubens. Fortunately it was not stolen in the war, either by the retreating Russians or by the invading Germans.

From Owen Rutter, The New Baltic States, *pub 1925*

not have any sense of design and there are no new booklets or postcards for visitors to buy. The general visitor will find the gloomy environment oppressive but specialists interested in stuffed animals, butterflies or stamps with natural history motifs should definitely come.

A little further along, at Laisvės 102, is the **main post office**, an enormous granite building dating inevitably from 1931 but with plenty of local wooden decoration as part of the interior. The stamps exhibited cover such diverse themes as Lithuanian industrial products, medieval kings, flowers, fire-engines and Chiune Sugihara, the Japanese Consul in Kaunas in 1940 who disobeyed his government by issuing thousands of visas which enabled local Jews to escape the Holocaust. Sets of stamps and first-day covers are also for sale here. The post office has a large Internet centre open daily from 08.00 to 20.00 which charges only about £0.40/$0.70 an hour. Beside this building is a statue of **Vytautas the Great**, stamping on his enemies, which was unveiled on 23 August 1990, a year before Lithuania's most recent enemy, the USSR, collapsed. It was a copy of an original by the sculptor Vincas Grybas (1890–1941). He was in fact a communist and the Germans murdered him as soon as they occupied Kaunas. Despite this, the Russians still removed the statue because of its unacceptable theme. The open space on the other side of the road is a commemoration garden for Romas Kalanta, a student aged 19 who burnt himself to death here in 1972 as a protest against the Soviet occupation. Details of this quickly spread abroad, although nothing could, of course, be said about it publicly in Lithuania at the time. The memorial, made up of 19 stones to represent one for every year of his life, was carved in 2002 to commemorate the 30th anniversary of his death.

Laisvės comes to an end with a large square dominated from the centre by the **Church of St Michael the Archangel.** As in other major Baltic cities, the Tsarist regime built imposing orthodox cathedrals in the late 19th century as part of their Russification campaigns. Ironically, by 1944, these churches were one of the few legacies that could not be destroyed by the new Soviet regime. During their occupation of Kaunas the building became a museum for stained glass and when independence was restored in 1990, the building was given to the Catholic Church, not to an orthodox community. In the crypt the **Museum for the Blind** opened in 2005 (*open daily 08.00–16.00*). It is based solely on sound, smell and touch. The first exhibition entitled 'Catacombs of the 21st century' will stay until 2008.

On the west side of the square is the **Mykolas Žilinskas Art Gallery** (*open Tue–Sun 11.00–17.00*). The building dates from the late Soviet period and it was to house the foreign art collection then held by the Čiurlionis Museum. However, Mykolas Žilinskas (1904–92) who fled from Lithuania in 1940 to what would become West Berlin, kindly donated his personal collection to Kaunas in the 1970s. He insisted that he would only donate it to Kaunas, to prevent the Russians taking it to Moscow. In exile he assembled a large collection of 16th–20th-century paintings and porcelain, which now form the basis of what is displayed here. It is supplemented by some Lithuanian paintings and by a Rubens picture of the Crucifixion. Of political interest are the Soviet items from the 1920s where designs from earlier periods are 'enhanced' with slogans. The tall statue of a male nude in front of the gallery continues to cause the controversy which was presumably its initial aim.

Unity Square (Vienybės Aikštė)

Vienybės aikštė is to the north of Laisvės, at its eastern end. Two universities and the Military Museum surround it. It is here that Lithuania commemorated its

Kaunas

founding, with statues of all those most active in the struggle for independence. Lenin, of course, took their place during the Soviet era but the originals were restored as much as possible immediately independence was restored.

When built in 1936, the **Military Museum** (*open Wed–Sun 11.00–18.00*), was the largest museum in Lithuania and it is pictured on the current 20 litas note. The architect Karolis Reisonas always built on a grand scale as is also clear from his Church of the Resurrection (see opposite). The collection covers all of the bitter wars fought on its territory. For foreigners, the Napoleonic rooms are probably those of most interest since there is extensive coverage of his advance through, and then quick retreat from Lithuania during his unsuccessful 1812 campaign against the Russians. For local people, greatest interest is shown in the crashed remains of the plane piloted across the Atlantic by Steponas Darius and Stasys Girėnas in July 1923 who just failed to reach Kaunas after a 37-hour flight. All sorts of memorabilia linked with them and with their fatal journey are also displayed.

Although almost totally unknown in the English-speaking world, Mikalojus Čiurlionis (1875–1911) would probably have become a world-famous figure had he lived longer or if Lithuanian independence had come about a few years earlier. He is both Lithuania's most famous composer and the country's most famous artist. He suffered all his life from physical and mental illness so viewing his painting and listening to his music is a melancholic but moving experience. Both are possible in the **Čiurlionis Art Museum** (*www. ciurlionis.lt; open Tue–Sun*

11.00–17.00) which bears his name and which is situated just behind the Military Museum. It is hard to believe that all the paintings on display here date from the last ten years of his life. The part of the museum where his work is displayed dates from 2003, so is well lit and ventilated. It is, however, worth visiting the rest of the building which has an extensive collection of wooden carvings, mainly from the 17th–19th centuries.

On leaving these austere surroundings, the **Devils Museum** (*open Tue–Sun 11.00–17.00*) over the road provides light relief, except perhaps in the depiction of Hitler and Stalin stamping over Lithuania. 'Devil' in the context of this museum could perhaps better be translated as 'joker' or as 'trickster'. The original owner died in 1966, but his spirit of fun lived on and now more than 2,000 little devils are on display. Perhaps the museum proves that it was possible to survive with a sense of humour through the Soviet occupation.

Beyond Unity Square

One of the two funicular railways in the town goes up to the **Church of the Resurrection**, on Green Hill. It dominates Kaunas which was clearly the aim of the architect Karolis Reisonas who won a competition for his design. Like so many other buildings that date from the 1930s, it reflects the need the town by then felt to operate on the basis of it being the permanent capital. Its size probably made it the largest building in the Baltics at the time. As many as 3,000 people could stand indoors and another 2,000 on the roof. However, it was never properly completed before the Soviet invasion in 1940 and was converted into a radio factory after their return in 1944. They obviously hoped that people would forget why it was originally built; that it was not mentioned in Soviet guidebooks is hardly surprising but it was still completely ignored during the early 1990s and only when fundraising started in earnest did it get noticed and visited again. Thick whitewash now covers the exterior and total emptiness greets the visitor indoors. In early 2005, there was no woodwork, no seating and no stained glass but doubtless the money for these will be found in due course. It is worth taking the lift up the 70m-high tower for the view over Kaunas.

The walk down Žemaičiu should be considered as an alternative to using the funicular again. At the foot of the hill, it becomes Vytauto which finishes at the railway station. The park here was largely created out of two former cemeteries, a Tartar one and a Lithuanian one both of which the Soviets cleared away in the 1960s. The park provided a backcloth for several revolutionary statues which are now in Grutas Park, the centre for Soviet sculpture near Druskininkai. The **mosque** built here in 1933 still exists although it was not, of course, allowed to function as such in Soviet times, when it was converted into a sports hall. The final stop on the way back to the bus or railway station is at the **Deportation Museum** (*open Wed–Sat 10.00–16.00*), a collection of documents and photographs about the thousands of Lithuanians deported to Siberia. This took place in two main 'waves', one just before the German invasion in June 1941 and the other in March 1949.

Beyond Kaunas

There are many worthwhile visits near to Kaunas which tourists staying longer than a day can make. Buses to most places leave from the main bus station, but quite a few also use the bus station beside the castle which is where to catch bus 24 to the **9th Fort**. The fort (*www.9fmuziejus.ot.lt; open daily except Tue 10.00–18.00*), 5km to the west of the town centre, was the last of a ring of forts around Kaunas to be built and it was completed in 1902. During World War II it became a major site for Holocaust atrocities. Not only was the local Jewish community murdered here, but so were many prisoners brought from France. Some of the cells have been kept exactly as there were during the war, with even graffiti still being visible. One prisoner wrote: '*Nous sommes 5,000 Français*' ('We are 5,000 French people'). In common with other camps in the Baltics, prisoners were shot rather than gassed and, given the proximity of this fort to the town, knowledge of what was happening there must have been commonplace in the town. Amazingly in the early Soviet period, the fort remained in use as a prison and Lithuanian partisans were executed here.

The Pažaislis Monastery (*open Mon–Sat 10.00–17.00*) is all the more imposing because it is so unexpected. A dreary 7km journey eastwards from the bus station on trolleybus 5 through Soviet suburbs and then to a small marina does not normally lead to an explosion of Baroque. Here it does, both inside and outside. No Lithuanian artist came near the building. Only Italians worked on it, hence the extensive use of black marble. It is fortunate that the centrepiece of the church being a tall hexagonal cupola has meant that much of the original paintwork survived, however irreligious subsequent owners may have been. Building began in the late 17th century on behalf of the Camaldolese order, an offshoot of the Benedictines who were accepted in the Polish–Lithuanian Commonwealth but hardly anywhere else outside Italy. The building was at peace throughout the 18th century but would then suffer nearly 200 years of tragedy. Napoleon's troops looted it in 1812; in 1832 it was closed following the anti-Tsarist demonstrations of the previous year and then passed to Russian Orthodox monks who removed the altars and painted over some of the frescoes. As the Tsarist forces retreated in 1915, they took what they could to Russia. Whilst nuns could return between 1920 and 1940, during the wars and in the early Soviet period the building was a hospital, a store, a home for the elderly and finally an art museum. To be fair to the Soviets, restoration did start in 1967 but it was only completed in the mid 1990s by which time, of course, nuns had returned.

The **Rumšiškės Open-Air Museum** is 18km east of Kaunas, and 2km south of the Vilnius–Kaunas highway. A direct bus leaves Kaunas bus station every 30 minutes for Rumšiškės. Buses on the highway are also prepared to stop at the Rumšiškės junction, from where it is necessary to walk (*open May–Sep Tue–Sun 10.00–18.00*). It has brought together about 180 buildings from all over the Lithuanian countryside since opening in 1974. They all date from between 1750 and 1950 and bearing in mind the 60,000 artefacts contained within them, there is no aspect of Lithuanian life which has not been covered. The museum is divided into four ethnographic areas and the inclusion of many farm animals, trees and plants ensures that the original settings are reproduced as accurately as possible. Visitors are unlikely to resent the demonstrations of handicrafts since woodcarving, weaving, basket-making and pottery were regular activities throughout the Lithuanian countryside. Three hours is the minimum time needed to get round and see the major exhibits, but a full day is well worthwhile in good weather.

TRAKAI

Set on a slim peninsula between sparkling lakes and forests, the picturesque village of Trakai (*www.trakai.lt*) is reason alone to visit Lithuania. Its biggest attraction is the awe-inspiring Island Castle, a truly magical sight filled with enchanting medieval atmosphere. Wooden bridges connect the castle with the rest of the village and leaping from them into the clear water in summer is almost irresistible. Yachts for hire and paddle boats circle Lake Galvė's 21 islands.

The castle keeps its fairy-tale quality in the depths of winter under a thick blanket of snow, the villagers out ice-fishing and the landscape deserted, making the whole adventure of coming here infinitely more personal.

Trakai Castle

There is a distinctly exotic flavour to Trakai, thanks to the presence of the

Trakai

Karaites, a community of Turkic settlers whose ancestors were taken as bodyguards by Vytautas the Great on his march south to the Crimea in 1398. They had converted to a branch of reformed Judaism in the 8th century and their oriental-looking prayer house, or Kenessa, built in the 18th century, and a Karaite museum are located on Karaimų Street. Their characteristic, colourful wooden houses, each with gable ends and three windows facing the street, line Karaimų. Perhaps the Karaites' most lasting legacy in Lithuania is culinary – the ubiquitous 'kibinai', Cornish-pasty-shaped pastries filled with juicy meat.

Transport

The 25km journey from Vilnius by bus or by train takes around 30 minutes. You might even take the bus in one direction and the train in the other, since the stations stand close together in both Vilnius and Trakai. A local bus covers the 2km between the bus station and the footbridge to the castle, but the walk through the village is much more pleasurable. Renting a car for the day is more advisable than hiring a taxi, since this will give the freedom to explore the beautiful surrounding landscape. Parking near the castle costs 5Lt.

Eating and drinking

Lunch or dinner in Trakai is now an appetising prospect. The range of restaurants has improved considerably since 2004, most serving traditional Lithuanian and Karaim food.

Trakai

Akmeninė Užeiga On the Vievis road, 2km from Trakai; ℩ (8-614) 86654

Oddly, this enviably situated restaurant, hotel, sauna and wine cellar on the shores of Lake Akmena, arguably the most beautiful body of water in Trakai, is not signposted at all. But that makes it one of the best-kept dining secrets in the country. Find it after turning right on the roundabout on the far side of Trakai. Pass the lake, climb a slope and it's on the left. It's a fabulous spot to dine, with two tables out on a pier on the water and more on the grassy bank with a fine view of the lake. Try the 'Baked pike-perch with Indonesian sauce', 'Fresh salmon Tatar' or the mouthwatering 'Braised mussels in mustard sauce'.

Apvalaus Stalo Klubas Karaimų 53a; ℩ (8-528) 55595

The strangely named Round Table Club is a classy restaurant on the quayside directly facing the Island Castle. It has both a formal dining room that is frequently empty and a pizza restaurant popular with the masses. The formal section serves particularly good fish dishes.

Csarda Aukštadvario 28a; ℩ (8-616) 55366

A Hungarian restaurant in Trakai is curious enough, but its location beside a busy Leader Price superstore when there are so many appealing locations for miles around is positively bizarre. Since the terrace overlooks the parking area, winter is a far more appealing season to dine here, the cosy tavern-like interior based around a central fireplace. The food? Not bad, and reasonably priced.

Kibininė Karaimų 65; ℩ (8-528) 55865

This long-standing Karaite restaurant with dark, barn-style interior has achieved cult status due to the fact that only two dishes have ever been on the menu – 'kibinai', of course, and a meat-and-veg stew served in a clay pot. Order both, since they are equally delicious, and why not wash them down with Lithuanian vodka.

Kiubėtė Vytauto 3a; ↘ (8-528) 59160
Situated on Lake Totoriškių, just off the beaten tourist path, the big attraction here is the unique pie that this charming, authentic Karaite restaurant is named after. The tasty traditional dish comes from old recipes handed down from owner Ingrida Špakovskaja's great-grandparents. Ingrida is one of the few remaining Karaim still living in Trakai.

Žvejų Namai On the Trakai road, 2km from Vievis; ↘ (8-528) 26008
At the 'home of the fishermen' don't go looking for veal. It's fish on the menu. And only fish. And only one kind of fish: trout. Catch your fish and order it cooked in the style of your choice – trout Mexican, trout Scottish, salted trout, rapidly salted trout, trout soup, it's up to you. A kilo of fish costs 29Lt, whichever way it's prepared.

What to see and do
The spectacular **Island Castle** dates from the 14th century, but was partially destroyed with Russia's invasion in 1655. From a distance, the extensive renovation work done between 1951 and 1962 – with Kremlin money, astonishingly enough, repairing a symbol of serfdom and national identity at the height of Soviet repression – appears to have been an amazing success. Up close, however, the lack of harmony between the original lumps of stone and modern factory-made bricks is obvious. But it is the awesome view of the castle from afar

Trakai

that all visitors remember, a sight that must have shaken the knees of any potential attacker.

When it was constructed on a cluster of three small islands, the 4m-thick walls literally rose up from the water. Every man coming to Trakai was ordered to bring a stone the size of a sheep's head or larger. The 30m-high keep was the residence of the Grand Duke, connected to the rest of the castle by a drawbridge. Steps leading down to the water where a boat was waiting was a possible secret escape in time of battle.

Vytautas the Great's escape from the Island Castle was far more remarkable, however. His ambitious cousins Jogaila and Skirgaila had taken it as theirs and then tricked Vytautas and his father Kęstutis into coming to negotiate for it, imprisoning them in the castle dungeon. Vytautas was a rare man in those days, wearing his hair long but without a beard. One night, his brave wife Anna, in the company of a serf girl, demanded to see her husband. Vytautas and the girl switched clothes, and the future grand duke slipped away undetected. When the cousins learned of this illustrious escape, they had both Kęstutis and the poor serf girl killed.

There were, in fact, three castles in Trakai. The ruins of the older **Peninsula Castle** can be strolled round or clambered over, a short walk upshore from the first bridge to the Island Castle. Covering 4ha, with 11 towers rising above the treeline, this was one of the biggest castles in the region. One story goes that it was built because Kęstutis's wife Birutė, the headstrong girl whom the impetuous grand duke had abducted as a pagan flame-tending maiden, wanted a bigger house. But thanks to the Christian Crusaders, it was badly damaged in 1390, just eight years after it was completed. Vytautas repaired it, but it was finally destroyed by the Russians in 1655.

All that remains of **Senieji Trakai** (literally Old Trakai), the first castle known to be built in Trakai, is a circular mound, at the centre of which now stands an 18th-century neo-Gothic church. This wooden castle was Kęstutis's residence and Vytautas's birthplace, built by Grand Duke Gediminas early in the 14th century. It can be found 3km from the town by taking a signposted lane to the left after exiting Trakai on the road back to Vilnius.

Walking away from the Island Castle down Karaimų, a track leading left after a short bridge leads to the haunting **Karaite Graveyard**. In contrast to the pristine cemeteries of the Lithuanians, this one is captivatingly overgrown, the headstones disappearing into the grass on the edge of the lake. It is a Karaite tradition to pray while touching the grave with a tissue, but it is also important to let nature take its course around the stone rather than keep it prim and tidy. After this, wander a few steps further up Karaimų and indulge in the Karaite dining experience at Kibininė.

Back in the other direction, past the castle, the **Karaite Museum** can be found at Karaimų 22. It is a fascinating mishmash of evocative old photographs, jewellery and a few weapons too. The community's 18th-century Kenessa stands nearby, on the same side of the street.

Further on, the little-visited, slightly shabby **Church of the Visitation** stands away from the road on a quiet hill. Originally dating from the time of Vytautas the

Trakai

Great though extensively altered in 1718, it is the unassuming home for an extraordinary painting of the Madonna and Child, also known as the **Madonna of Trakai**. Said to be a gift from a Byzantine emperor to Vytautas the Great, this is unlikely, it probably dating from the 16th century, its silver covering added in the 18th, as was the fashion.

Information and maps

Historical National Park Information Centre Karaimų 5; ☎ (8238) 55776. Maps of the town and its attractions are available. Open Mon–Thu 08.00–12.00 and 12.45–17.00, Fri 08.00–12.00 and 12.45–15.00.

Tourist Information Centre Vytauto 69; ☎/f(8238) 51934; e trakaiTIC@is.lt; www.trakai.lt. Some English is spoken. Open in summer Mon–Fri 09.00–18.00, Sat 10.00–15.00; in winter Mon–Fri 08.00–17.00.

KERNAVĖ

The first capital of the united Lithuanian tribes is about 50km northwest on Vilnius. It can be driven to on a leisurely minor road that stretches through rolling countryside beyond the capital's outer suburb of Pilaitė. There are several places to stop along the way. **Sudervė** is a lovely village beside a lake that is dominated by a unique round church designed by Laurynas Stuoka-Gucevičius (1753–98), the young classical architect who also redesigned Vilnius Cathedral.

Further down the road, an old **oak wood and runic stone** can be explored near Dūkštos (find the roadside sign saying *ažuolynas*). A trail leads between these majestic oaks, while the mysterious stone with its so-far-untranslated runic script probably dates from the 3rd or 4th century AD, the time when Goths established their dominions across whole swathes of Eastern Europe.

Kernavė (www.kernave.org) is a tiny village set on a terrace above the green and grassy valley of the River Neris. The reason for visiting is a series of five mounds at the ridge of the valley that hint at a lost city. An observation platform and information point reveal the whole panorama, from which you are free to descend into the landscape and explore. Each mound has a name, not all of them accurate. The wooden castle that once stood here rested on Mindaugas's Throne Mound, whereas Castle Mound was more likely to have been home to quite a sizeable medieval population. A Lithuanian pagan mystic named Lizdeika was said to have lived on Hearth Mound, always tending a sacred flame. But Lizdeika Mound probably had a defensive purpose. Confusing? An excellent archaeological museum adjacent to the site provides plenty of explanatory information, but unfortunately it is closed for extensive renovation until 2008. However, the excellent website above compensates for this temporary loss.

Archaeological finds have determined that the site was inhabited in the Neolithic period, as far back as 9000BC. The peaceful pagan town and trading centre that prospered here in the Middle Ages was raided, ransacked and badly damaged by Crusaders in 1365, then again in 1390. It never recovered after the second blow and gradually vanished. The mighty army of Crusaders from western Europe who

Kernavė

dealt it consisted of mercenaries from Germany, France, Italy and England – including the future Henry IV. This was the army that marched on to Vilnius to inflict such devastation on the Crooked Castle and the Upper Castle.

Tourist Information Centre Kerniaus 4; ☏ (8-382) 4731;
e kernave@taigaeurobaltika.com. Some English is spoken. Open May–Sep, 10.00–18.00 except Sun.

Higher Castle

Language

ALPHABET

The Lithuanian alphabet is as follows (with letters in the order shown):

a ą b c č d e ę ė f g h i į y j k l m n o p r s š t u ų ū v z ž

If using a Lithuanian dictionary or directory, beware that these are all considered separate letters in their own right. This means, for example, that a word beginning Ša will appear after one beginning Su, and that ch and y are in different positions from in English.

PRONUNCIATION

Vowel sounds can be either short or long: the accented letters have the general effect of lengthening the sound of the comparable unaccented letter.

a	as in **a**mount	i	as in s**i**t
ą	as in f**a**ther	į or y	as in f**ee**t
e	as in m**e**t	o	as in b**oa**t
ę	as in **a**mber	u	as in p**u**t
ė	as in p**ai**r	ū or ų	as in s**ue**

Common diphthongs are

ai	as in **ai**sle	ie	as in y**e**t
au	as in **ou**t	ui	as in ph**ooey**
ei	as in m**ay**	uo	as in the Italian b**uo**no

The consonants b, d, f, g, h, k, l, m, n, p, s, t, v and z are pronounced approximately the same way as in English, but the following have a different sound:

c	as **ts**, as in an**ts**	j	as the letter **y**, as in **y**es
č	as **ch**, as in **ch**op	r	is always trilled or rolled
ch	as in the Scottish lo**ch**	š	as **sh**, as in **sh**ip
dž	as the letter **j**, as in **j**am	ž	as the letter **s**, as in mea**s**ure

USEFUL WORDS AND EXPRESSIONS
Greetings and civilities

Hello	*Laba diena*	Excuse me, sorry	*Atsiprašau*
Hi	*Labas, Sveikas*	How are you?	*Kaip sekasi?*
Good morning	*Labas rytas*	OK	*Gerai*
Good evening	*Labas vakaras*	Cheers	*Į, Sveikatą*
Goodnight	*Labanakt*	Do you speak English?	*Ar kalbate angliškai?*
Goodbye	*Viso gero*	I don't speak	*Aš nekalbu*
See you soon	*Iki pasimatymo*		

Language

Please	*Prašau*	Lithuanian	*lietuviškai*
Thank you	*Ačiū*	I don't understand	*Aš nesuprantu*

Basic words

yes	*taip*	departure	*išvyksta,*
no	*ne*		*išvykimo laikas*
open	*atidaryta*	ticket	*bilietas*
closed	*uždaryta*	ticket office	*kasa*
entrance	*įėjimas*	now	*dabar*
exit	*išėjimas*	today	*šandien*
arrival	*atvyksta, atvykimo laikas*	yesterday	*vakar*
tomorrow	*rytoj*		
daily	*kasdien*	small	*mažas*
big	*didelis*		

Basic questions and requests

When?	*Kada?*	May I have the bill?	*Prašyčiau sąskaitą?*
Where?	*Kur?*		
Who?	*Kas?*	I would like ...	*Norėčiau ...*
Why?	*Kodėl?*	to order	*užsisakyti*
How much does it cost?	*Kiek kainuoja?*	a single room	*vienvietį kambarų*
		a double room	*dvivietį kambarų*
to go to ...	*nueiti ? ...*		

Directions

left	*kairė*	north	*šaurė*
right	*dešinė*	south	*pietūs*
back	*atgal*	east	*rytai*
straight ahead	*tiesiai*	west	*vakarai*

Locations

airport	*aerouostas*	bus station	*autobusų stotis*
beach	*pliažas*	café	*kavinė*
bookshop	*knygynas*	castle	*pilis*
bridge	*tiltas*	cathedral	*katedra*
cemetery	*kapinės*	museum	*muziejus*
church	*bažnyčia*	pharmacy	*vaistinė*
currency exchange	*valiutos keitykla*	post office	*paštas*
forest	*miškas*	railway station	*geležinkelio stotis*
harbour	*uostas*	restaurant	*restoranas*
hill	*kalnas*	river	*upė*
hospital	*ligoninė*	road	*kelias*
hotel	*viešbutis*	square	*aikštė*
lake	*ežeras*	street	*gatvė*
market	*turgus*	theatre	*teatras*

Language

Numbers

0	*nulis*	15	*penkiolika*
1	*vienas*	16	*šešolika*
2	*du*	17	*septyniolika*
3	*trys*	18	*aštuoniolika*
4	*keturi*	19	*devyniolika*
5	*penki*	20	*dvidešimt*
6	*šeši*	30	*trisdešimt*
7	*septyni*	40	*keturiasdešimt*
8	*aštuoni*	50	*penkiasdešimt*
9	*devyni*	60	*šešasdešimt*
10	*dešimt*	70	*septyniasdešimt*
11	*vienuolika*	80	*aštuoniasdešimt*
12	*dvylika*	90	*devyniasdešimt*
13	*trylika*	100	*šimtas*
14	*keturiolika*	1,000	*tūkstantis*

Days of the week

Monday	*pirmadienis*	Friday	*penktadienis*
Tuesday	*antradienis*	Saturday	*šeštadienis*
Wednesday	*trečiadienis*	Sunday	*sekmadienis*
Thursday	*ketvirtadienis*		

Useful words and expressions

Months

January	*sausis*	July	*liepa*
February	*vasaris*	August	*rugpjūtis*
March	*kovas*	September	*rugsėjis*
April	*balandis*	October	*spalis*
May	*gegužė, gegužis*	November	*lapkritis*
June	*birželis*	December	*gruodis*

Language

Further information

BOOKS
Published outside Lithuania

Jewish history has been well covered by publishers in the UK and USA, but there is still very little published on other topics. The following provide useful background to a visit to Vilnius.

Bouchet, Stephane *Mort à Vilnius* Archipel 2004. Readers of French will be interested in the background to the most celebrated murder probably ever committed in Vilnius. In July 2003 one of France's best-known film actresses, Marie Trintignant, was mortally wounded there by her lover Bertrand Cantat while she was working on a film about the novelist Colette.

Collishaw, Stephan *The Lost Girl* Sceptre 2003. Set in Vilnius at various times during the 20th century. His second novel, *Amber*, is set partly in Vilnius and partly in Afghanistan.

Good, Michael *The Search for Major Plagge* Fordham University Press 2005. Describes his research to track down the story of this SS Officer who saved at least a thousand Jews in Vilnius during the German occupation between 1941 and 1944.

Hiden, John and Salmon, Patrick *The Baltic Nations and Europe* Longman 1994. Compares the three Baltic states during their first independence period and then under the Soviet occupation.

Landsbergis, Vytautas *Lithuania, Independent Again* University of Wales 2000. Autobiographical account. Landsbergis led Lithuania to independence and is currently (2005) an MEP. It is particularly graphic about the struggles in 1990 and 1991 to break away from the USSR before it collapsed of its own accord.

Milosz, Czeslaw *Native Realm: A Search for Self-Definition* Farrar, Straus and Giroux 2002. A fascinating autobiography of this 1980 Nobel Prize winner for literature, a search for self-identity that contains some evocative images from the early 20th century.

Shneidman, N N *Jerusalem of Lithuania* Mosaic 1998. Shneidman survived the Holocaust in Vilnius and lived there until 1957. The book therefore also covers the history of the tiny Jewish community that remained after the War.

Thomson, Clare *The Singing Revolution* Michael Joseph 1992. Describes the author's travels through the Baltic states just before the collapse of the USSR.

Published in Lithuania

Kubilius, Vytautas *Adam Mickiewicz* Leidykla 1998. A short biography on the early 19th-century Polish/Lithuanian writer who is probably the most famous literary figure ever to have lived in Vilnius, although much of his work had to be written in exile in France.

Lithuania on the Map National Museum of Lithuania 2002. A catalogue published originally by the National Museum for an exhibition held in 1999, but it is still on sale and vividly brings to life through centuries of maps, the political struggles Lithuania has had to endure.

Potašenko, Grigorijus *The Peoples of the Grand Duchy of Lithuania* Aidai 2002. Background on all the main ethnic and religious groups that make up contemporary Vilnius including the Tatars and the Roma.

Revival of Lithuanian Cultural Heritage Describes and illustrates the extent of their work which covers funicular railways and abandoned factories just as much as Baroque churches.

Venclova, Tomas *Vilnius* Paknio 2002. This is the book with which every tourist returns from Vilnius. The author was expelled from Vilnius in the late 1970s for his dissident writing and is now a Professor at Yale. It is updated each year, both in the text and with its lavish photographs. Particularly worthy of note is the description he gives of Vilnius before the War, when it was occupied by the Poles.

Vilnius Views of the Past and Present Darlis 2003. Photographs of Vilnius comparing the early and late 20th century.

Zamoyski, Adam *1812: Napoleon's Fatal March to Moscow* Harper Perennial 2004. Graphic and pitiful description of the Grand Armée's tragic retreat, during which thousands died in and around Vilnius.

WEBSITES

Websites of specific interest are detailed at the appropriate point in the text. The following are worth consulting for more general information in English.

http://ausis.gf.vu.lt/eka Fascinating journey through Lithuanian culture and traditions, prepared by Vilnius University.

www.akropolis.lt Tourists from neighbouring countries often spend their whole stay in Lithuania at this shopping complex and leisure centre. Others may want to use the website to find a specific shop, book a session on the ice-rink or see what is on at one of the eight different cinemas.

www.balticsww.com Listings, info and articles old and new from the Baltic-wide magazine *City Paper*.

www.bradtguides.com Updates on this book and other Bradt Baltic guides will be regularly supplied here.

www.britain.lt British Embassy website with details of the links between Britain and Lithuania.

www.catholic.lt Services and other events taking place in Catholic churches.

www.club.lt A guide to all the nightclubs in Vilnius.

www.culture.lt A website covering all aspects of the arts in Lithuania.

www.eurolines.lt Timetables for international buses to and from Vilnius.

www.inyourpocket.com Contains most of the text of the current edition of the *Vilnius in Your Pocket* and *Kaunas in Your Pocket* guides, with up-to-date information on hotels, restaurants, airlines and bus connections .

www.kaunas.lt The official website of the city of Kaunas.

www.ldm.lt The website of the Applied Arts Museum, the Radvila Palace and Vilnius Picture Gallery, with full details of current exhibitions.

www.lithuanianinstitute.lt Details on the organisation charged with promoting Lithuania abroad, including details of their publications.

www.litjews.org Information on the Jewish community in Vilnius.

www.litrail.lt The website of the railway network, complete with timetables and route-planning information.

www.lnm.lt The website of the Lithuanian National Museum, their collections and publications.

www.maps.lt A website offering comprehensive cartographic coverage of Lithuania.

www.muziejai.lt Comprehensive information about every museum in Lithuania can be found on this website.

www.online.lt An umbrella website for a wide range of information on Lithuania.

www.post.lt Details of all postage charges from Lithuania.

www.shoah.smm.lt Resource for Holocaust research.

www.std.lt This website is the place to look for all sorts of official statistics about Lithuania.

www.toks.lt Timetables of buses between Vilnius and other towns in Lithuania.

www.travel.lt The site of the Lithuanian Tourist Board.

www.urm.lt The website of the Ministry of Foreign Affairs gives up-to-date information on visas, customs regulations, Lithuanian embassies abroad and foreign embassies based in Vilnius.

www.vilnius.lt The official website of the city of Vilnius.

www.vilius-airport.lt Details of current airline schedules, arrival/departure information, and all airport offices and facilities.

Websites

www.vilniustransport.lt Full timetables for local buses and trolleybuses.
www.vu.lt Vilnius University, including its history and collections.
www.wifi.lt Directory for wireless Internet access points.

Trakai Castle

Index

208

index

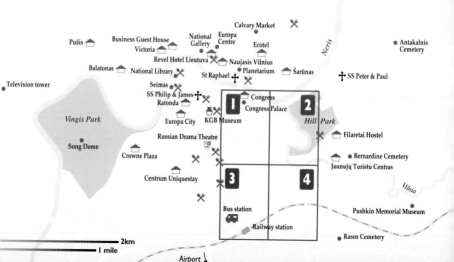

VILNIUS

© Bradt Travel Guides Ltd

N
Bradt

Le Meridien Villon Resort

Siemens Arena

Akropolis Shopping Centre

Šaltoniškių
Cemetery

Calvary Market

Pušis

Business Guest House   National   Europa
Victoria   Gallery   Centre   Ecotel

Antakalnis
Cemetery

Revel Hotel Lieutuva   Naujasis Vilnius
Balatonas   National Library   St Raphael   Planetarium   Šarūnas
                                                                                        SS Peter & Paul

Television tower

Seimas
SS Philip & James
Ratonda

Congress
Congress Palace

Europa City   KGB Museum

Russian Drama Theatre

Vingis Park

Hill Park

Filaretai Hostel

Song Dome

Crowne Plaza

Bernardine Cemetery
Jaunujų Turistu Centras

Centrum Uniquestay

Vilnia

Bus station

Pushkin Memorial Museum

Railway station

Rasos Cemetery

Neris

0 ──────── 2km
0 ──────── 1 mile

Airport

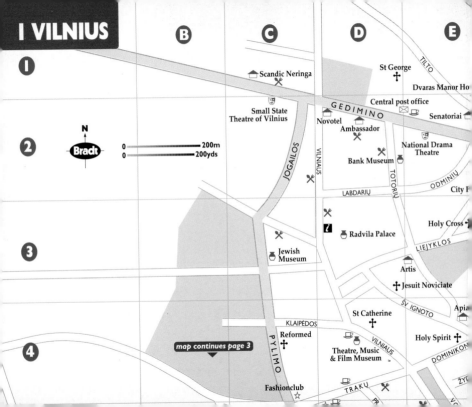

1 VILNIUS

A   **B**   **C**   **D**   **E**

1

Scandic Neringa

St George ✝

Dvaras Manor Ho

Central post office

GEDIMINO

Senatoriai

Small State
Theatre of Vilnius

Novotel

Ambassador

National Drama
Theatre

2

Bradt

0   200m
0   200yds

N

Bank Museum

ODMINIŲ

City P

LABDARIŲ

JOGAILOS

VILNIAUS

TOTORIŲ

3

Holy Cross ✝

LIEJYKLOS

Jewish
Museum

Radvila Palace

Artis

✝ Jesuit Noviciate

SV. IGNOTO

Apia

4

KLAIPĖDOS

St Catherine ✝

map continues page 3

PYLIMO

Reformed ✝

Theatre, Music
& Film Museum

Holy Spirit ✝

VILNIAUS

DOMINIKON

Fashionclub

TRAKŲ

ŽY

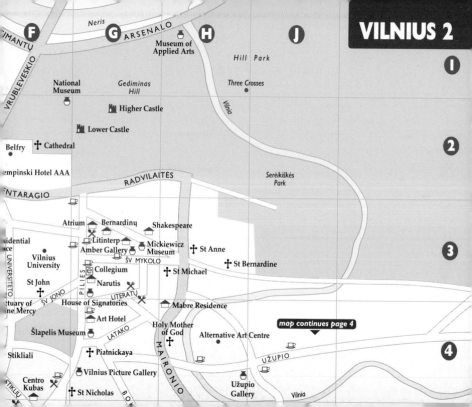

F

G ARSENALO

H

J

I

Neris

Museum of
Applied Arts

Hill Park

Three Crosses

National
Museum

Gediminas
Hill

Vilnia

Higher Castle

2

Lower Castle

Belfry

Cathedral

empinski Hotel AAA

RADVILAITĖS

Sereikiškės
Park

NTARAGIO

UNIVERSITETO

Atrium

Bernardinų

Shakespeare

Litinterp

Mickiewicz
Museum

St Anne

3

Amber Gallery

ŠV MYKOLO

St Bernardine

idential
ce

Vilnius
University

Collegium

St Michael

St John

Narutis

PILIES

ŠV JONO

LITERATŲ

tuary of
ne Mercy

House of Signatories

Mabre Residence

map continues page 4

Art Hotel

LATAKO

Holy Mother
of God

Alternative Art Centre

Šlapelis Museum

MAIRONIO

UŽUPIO

4

Stikliai

Piatnickaya

Centro
Kubas

Vilnius Picture Gallery

St Nicholas

B.O

Užupio
Gallery

Vilnia

STIKLIŲ

3 VILNIUS

map continues page 1

The Assumption

Evangelical Lutheran

St Nicholas

KEY

Palace	
Castle	
Hotel	
Restaurant	
Café	
Internet café	
Nightclub	
Church	
Synagogue	
Museum/gallery	
Theatre	
Post office	
Bus station	
Railway station	

Tolerence Centre

NAUGARDUKO

AGUONU

AAA Mano Liza

Grotthuss

LIGONINES

PYLIMO

Synagogue

All S

Conti

RAUGYKLOS

SV STEPONO

GELIU

Comfort

SODU

AAA Hostel

ŠOPENO

Panoram

© Bradt Travel Guides Ltd

Bus station

A B C D E

Kubas

St Nicholas

SAVIČIAUS

BOKŠTO

Gallery

Vilnia

Čiurlionis House

St Mary the Soothing

Kazys Varnelis House Museum

ROTUŠĖS AIKŠTĖ

map continues page 2

Town hall

Barbacan Palace

Contemporary Arts Centre

St Casimir

SV KAZIMIERO

Artillery Bastion

SUBAČIAUS

Radisson SAS Astorija

Assumption

Lėlė Puppet Theatre & Youth Theatre

Ramada

DIDŽIOJI

Grybas House

SUBAČIAUS

National Philharmonic Hall

Heart of Jesus

AUŠROS VARTŲ

Europa Royale

Arka Art Gallery

Holy Spirit

Tamsta

ARKLIŲ

Basilian Gate & Monastery

Domus Maria

DAUKŠOS

St Teresa

Gates of Dawn

BAZILIJONŲ

City Gate

Central Market

AUŠROS VARTŲ

Old Town Hostel

PYLIMO

Mikotel

GELEŽINKELIO

EINŲ

LIEPKALNIO

Railway station

F   **G**   **H**   **J**   **K**

5   6   7   8

View of Vilnius Old Town and Užupis, with Higher Castle in the background (GT)

Šv Kazimiero Street, Old Town (GT)

Pilies Street café culture (GT)

The glittering crown on St Casimir's Church (GT)

St Anne's Church (GT)

The Orthodox Church of the Holy Spirit (CN)

The angel of
Užupis (GT)

Statue of muses outside the
National Drama Theatre (CN)

Observatory, Vilnius
University (CN)